Anne Smi

1933-1939

Dick B
2005

Other Titles by Dick B.

Dr. Bob and His Library

The Oxford Group & Alcoholics Anonymous:
A Design for Living That Works

The Akron Genesis of Alcoholics Anonymous

New Light on Alcoholism:
The A.A. Legacy from Sam Shoemaker

The Books Early AAs Read for Spiritual Growth

Courage to Change (with Bill Pittman)

The Good Book and The Big Book:
A.A.'s Roots in the Bible

That Amazing Grace:
The Role of Clarence and Grace S. in Alcoholics Anonymous

Good Morning!:
Quiet Time, Morning Watch, Meditation, and Early A.A.

Turning Point:
A History of A.A.'s Spiritual Roots and Successes

HOPE!:
The Story of Geraldine D., Alina Lodge & Recovery

Utilizing Early A.A.'s Spiritual Roots for Recovery Today

Anne Smith's Journal 1933-1939

A.A.'s Principles of Success

Third Edition

Dick B.

Foreword by Bob S. ("Smitty"), Dr. Bob and Anne's son
Co-author, *Children of the Healer*

Paradise Research Publications, Inc.
Kihei, Maui, Hawaii

Paradise Research Publications, Inc., P.O. Box 837, Kihei, HI 96753-0837

 First edition 1992
Third edition 1998
Printed in the United States of America

This Paradise Research Publications, Inc., Edition is published by arrangement with Good Book Publishing Company, P.O. Box 837, Kihei, HI 96753-0837

Cover Design: Lili Crawford (Maui Cyber Design)

The publication of this volume does not imply affiliation with nor approval or endorsement from Alcoholics Anonymous World Services, Inc.

Publisher's Cataloging in Publication

B., Dick.
Anne Smith's journal, 1933-1939 : A.A.'s principles of success / Dick. B.--Rev. Paradise ed.
p. cm.
Includes bibliographical references and index.
ISBN: 1-885803-24-9
1. Smith, Anne R.--Diaries. 2. Alcoholics Anonymous--History. 3. Alcoholism--Treatment--United States. I. Title

HV5278.B17 1994 362.29287'092

(previously published by Good Book Publishing Company, ISBN: 1-881212-00-9; and Glen Abbey Books, ISBN: 0-934125-34-1; previous title: Anne Smith's Spiritual Workbook: An AA-Good Book Connection)

Library of Congress Catalog Card Number: 98-92158

"God is love"

"He that loveth not knoweth not God;
for God is love." (1 John 4:8)

Compare: *DR. BOB and the Good Oldtimers*, p. 117;
Not-God, p. 55.

"Faith without works is dead"

"For as the body without the spirit is dead,
so faith without works is dead also." (James 2:26)

Compare: *DR. BOB and the Good Oldtimers*, p. 71;
Alcoholics Anonymous (the "Big Book"), 3rd ed., pp. 14, 76, 88;
Pass It On, p. 147

To Betty Smith, daughter-in-law of Dr. Bob and Anne Smith

Contents

Foreword to the First Edition

As history evolves, there are a very few persons whose quiet, soft-spoken, anonymous activities, whose unfailing faith, whose deep spirituality, have aided in the recovery of millions of desperate human beings. The way that help was given, steadfast love was shown, was so subtle, so unassuming, so void of self seeking that only a few know of the debt that is owed.

Such a person was Anne Ripley Smith, my mother, beloved wife and partner of Dr. Bob, and truly the "mother of A.A."

Anne Robinson Ripley was born in Oak Park, Illinois, in 1891, one of four children, having three brothers. Early education completed in Oak Park, Anne entered Wellesley College on a scholarship, graduated, and entered the teaching profession. She married Dr. Bob Smith, an Akron physician and later surgeon, raised two children, a boy and a girl, and lived the balance of her life at 855 Ardmore Avenue in Akron, Ohio, the home that is now an historical monument as the birth place of A.A.

Never losing faith in her alcoholic husband, she turned to an organization called the Oxford Group, whose basic premise was basic, simple Christianity in an attempt to solve the dilemma of the practicing alcoholic who wanted desperately to quit drinking.

The author of this book, Dick B., has painstakingly researched the Oxford Group notebook Anne kept so faithfully, and, in doing so, has made the spiritual depth of that astonishing, lovely person available to all of us.

Although her three brothers each made "Who's Who in America" through their own work, this Anne and her contribution are timeless. I hope the reading of this book will deepen each reader's sense of infinite power that lies within each of us.

BOB S. ("SMITTY")

Preface to the Revised Paradise Edition

This book was the second of a series on the spiritual history of Alcoholics Anonymous, particularly as it emanated from the Bible and Christian roots. The first book, *Dr. Bob's Library*, listed, summarized, and commented on the immense number of spiritual books that A.A.'s co-founder, Dr. Robert Holbrook Smith, read as he and Bill Wilson were endeavoring to put together the spiritual recovery program that later was to be called A.A.'s Twelve Steps. The first printing of that book was sold out; so was the second. And it has been revised, with a new publisher. All our intended shorter books are but part of a major research project. The author has been researching the spiritual principles espoused by the Oxford Group, Dr. Samuel M. Shoemaker, Dr. Bob, Anne Smith (his wife), and Henrietta Seiberling. (Henrietta contributed much to the early spiritual education of Dr. Bob and Bill W.) The historical research work can be of value to AAs, Al-Anons, and other Twelve Step people in their spiritual growth. The author's books can be and are being used by study groups. They can be resources for those who speak on A.A.'s rich, religious heritage. And the books can be and are being used by churches, clergy, therapists, and counselors who need to speak to substance abusers and their families in terms of the early historical principles and practices, principles and practices which worked! Bill W. and Dr. Bob were clear that A.A.'s spiritual principles came from the Bible, the Oxford Group, and Rev. Sam Shoemaker. But neither gave details.

This book, *Anne Smith's Journal, 1933-1939*, analyzes a sixty-four-page journal which Dr. Bob's wife, Anne, compiled and her daughter, Sue, partially typed during A.A.'s formative period from 1933 to 1939. A.A. histories are clear that Anne was a major participant in the early spiritual education of Dr. Bob and Bill—particularly in the summer of 1935 when Bill lived with the Smiths. Bill called Anne the "Mother of A.A." But there has been no detailed information about Anne's beliefs, studies, discussions, or writings.

In the spring of 1991, the author became aware from his reading of Dr. Ernest Kurtz's *Not-God,* that Dr. Bob's wife, Anne, had written what Kurtz called an "Oxford Group Work-book." This seemed to open a door to what the Smiths and Wilson might have read, studied, and discussed about the Bible and in other spiritual reading in the summer of 1935—as well as before and after 1935. The author met with Dr. Bob's daughter, Sue Smith Windows, at Founders Day in Akron, Ohio, in June of 1991, and secured her written permission to obtain Anne Smith's spiritual notes from A.A.'s General Service Archives. A.A. Archives cooperated fully; and we carefully read and studied Anne's notes.

The material was astonishing. Anne had written at length on every single spiritual principle which became embodied in A.A.'s Twelve Steps. She covered much of the material one finds in A.A.'s basic text, *Alcoholics Anonymous*. She quoted rich material from the Bible and Christian literature. And she analyzed and wrote about every one of some twenty-eight Oxford Group principles the author had been studying and had reconstructed from his research. She also detailed a good deal of recommended spiritual reading—including the Bible itself. And Dr. Bob's daughter, Sue, established that Dr. Bob had read the books Anne recommended.

When all was said and done, it was clear to the author that Anne had written a compendium on Bible-Oxford Group-Shoemaker concepts, principles, and practices as she saw and endeavored to practice them in the 1930's. Since Dr. Bob and Bill had specified these as the major sources of A.A.'s spiritual program of recovery, Anne's work loomed large in our mind as a resource. It can and should indicate the source ideas that were arresting her attention; that probably were discussed at length with her husband, Dr. Bob; that definitely were shared with early AAs and their families in the Smith Home in Akron, where A.A. was born; and very likely were communicated to Bill—directly or indirectly. Thus an important, detailed source of Bill W.'s Big Book and Twelve Step ideas may exist in Anne Smith's Journal. We believe so.

A word about the Journal itself. A few parts are still in Anne's hand-writing and are very difficult to read. Some of the hand-written pages did not come out very well when they were copied for the author by A.A. General Services in New York; and these are somewhat difficult to read. Most of the notes were typed for Anne by her daughter, Sue; and there are a few discernable errors in the typing process. Also, some of the typed format did not lend itself well to our printed process; and we have taken the liberty of placing it in a more readable form, without in any way deleting words or phrases, or intending to detract from context and content. The pages we cite as Journal pages are not necessarily those which Anne used. They are the page numbers assigned to the copy sent to the author by A.A. General Services in New York; and the reader can always refer back to the original by using our pages and then comparing them with the identical pages in archives. A final note, also mentioned in our book: Sue Windows is convinced that some of the pages of her mother's original Journal are missing from the copies sent to her and to us. We have at least found a completeness in the works before us because they seem completely to address all matters in the Twelve Steps, most matters in A.A.'s Big Book, and all of the Oxford Group concepts we have found to have influenced A.A. We have seen the copies in the New York Archives, at Bill Wilson's Home at Stepping Stones, and in the possession of Dr. Bob's son, "Smitty," in Texas. And our work addresses the content in all of these copies.

Acknowledgements

As with my previous research, writing, and computer work on the A.A./Biblical roots project, my gratitude begins with my son, Ken. He is a first-rate scholar and Bible student; and he is computer literate. The experience he gained in all these areas in writing his Master's Thesis in the field of communication, in teaching communications and Bible subjects, and in his daily work in the computer industry were simply not available to me on my own. Through Ken, that experience was utilized in my work. Also, Ken has spent hours editing, formatting, helping, and encouraging.

There are some other major acknowledgments. The first is to Sue Smith Windows, Dr. Bob's daughter, who lives in Akron, Ohio. She opened part of Dr. Bob's Library to me (as did her brother, Robert, and his wife, Betty, at a later point). She spent hours in personal interviews, on the phone, in correspondence, in review of my manuscripts, and in her attic—searching. Her personal authorization enabled me to obtain the Anne Smith Journal pages from A.A. Archives in New York. Nell Wing—A.A.'s first archivist and Bill Wilson's secretary—facilitated. And Frank M., A.A.'s retired archivist in New York, has spent hours in personal conversations, phone calls, correspondence, and encouragement. He was the person who sent the Journal pages to Sue and to me.

Others who have reviewed, encouraged, criticized, and helped beyond measure are Dr. Ernest Kurtz, author of *Not-God: A History of Alcoholics Anonymous*; Garth D. Lean—Dr. Frank Buchman's biographer and prolific Oxford Group writer; the

Reverend T. Willard Hunter, longtime Oxford Group worker, leader, and speaker; Dr. Bob's entire family—Sue Smith Windows, Robert R. Smith, and Elizabeth Smith (Robert's wife); Henrietta Seiberling's children, former Congressman John F. Seiberling, and his sisters, Dorothy Seiberling and Mary Seiberling Huhn; Mrs. W. Irving Harris, widow of Dr. Sam Shoemaker's associate, the Reverend W. Irving Harris [Mrs. Harris was in charge of the Oxford Group "bookstore" at Shoemaker's Calvary Church, which bookroom was located at Calvary House in New York where Shoemaker and the Harrises lived]. Thanks to Oxford Group activists, the Reverend Harry J. Almond, Kenneth D. Belden, James Houck, Dr. Martin Morris, Michael Hutchinson, James D. Newton, Eleanor Forde Newton, L. Parks Shipley, Sr., and George Vondermuhll, Jr.. Thanks to Ray G., archivist at Dr. Bob's Home in Akron; Paul L., archivist at Bill W.'s Home at Stepping Stones in New York; and to Gail L., archivist at Akron's Founders Day activities. Joe McQ. and Charley P. of Arkansas, who have carried the Big Book message to many places, have offered great assistance and encouragement. Also, Tim M., who facilitated the Big Book Seminar in Sacramento, California. Charles Bishop, Jr.—"The Bishop of Books,"—publisher of my first title; Mel B., author of *New Wine: The Spiritual Roots of the Twelve Step Miracle*; and Dennis C., an A.A. historian and collector from Connecticut, have all been helpful in my work.

All these and others unmentioned have given me a new lease on life and a new purpose in it. A.A.'s Biblical roots needed to be uncovered, discovered, and disseminated, that others may use the early tools to grow; and the encouragement of others has been heartwarming. Among the others are my A.A. sponsor, Henry B.; a good many of the men I sponsor in A.A.; the participants in my Bible fellowship; and a large number of my A.A. friends in the California and Maui A.A. Fellowships. Also, a growing number around the U.S.

1

A Lady of Faith, Courage, and Love

The Need for a Revised Edition

The need for a revision of our first edition became ever more clear with each new bit of information that we unearthed over the past eight years of research and analysis.

Two A.A. historians recently called the journal Anne Ripley Smith kept during A.A.'s formative years, between 1933 and 1939, her "Oxford Group" workbook or notebook.[1] After carefully reviewing Anne's sixty-four pages of notes, we found they contained a good deal of information as to principles and practices of the Oxford Group, of which A.A. was a part at its inception. And Anne's daughter, Sue Smith Windows, has described Anne's journal as "Mom's notebook from the Oxford Group meetings."[2] *But Anne's notes covered far more than just Oxford Group material.* We therefore chose, in our first edition, to call Anne's writings "Anne Smith's Spiritual Workbook."

---

[1] See Ernest Kurtz, *Not-God: A History of Alcoholics Anonymous*. exp. ed. (Minnesota: Hazelden, 1991), p. 331, n32; Mary C. Darrah, *Sister Ignatia: Angel of Alcoholics Anonymous* (Chicago: Loyola University Press, 1992), pp. 115-16. Darrah referred to Anne's work as her "Oxford Group journal."

[2] Bob Smith and Sue Smith Windows, *Children of the Healer: The Story of Dr. Bob's Kids* (Illinois: Parkside Publishing Corporation, 1992), p. 29.

Despite our deletion of an Oxford Group reference from our first edition's title, we were still very much fascinated with Anne's focus on almost every Oxford Group principle that influenced A.A. We therefore devoted most of that edition to reviewing what the Oxford Group's principles were, and then illustrating how and where Anne had addressed or adopted them.

In the intervening years, however, we received many communications asking for more of what Anne *herself* had written. We have also confirmed that Anne shared the contents of her notebook with the many early AAs and families who lived at, or visited, the Smith home in Akron. And we have now concluded that Anne very probably shared her material with A.A.'s co-founders—Dr. Bob (her husband) and Bill Wilson. This particularly because Wilson lived with the Smiths for three months in 1935 when A.A.'s principles of recovery were being developed. Also, because Wilson himself spoke of Anne's reading to him and Dr. Bob from the Bible and other Christian literature each day during Bill's stay; and Anne's journal concerned Biblical/Christian literature she recommended for spiritual nourishment.

The author therefore re-examined the notebook, looking carefully for what Anne *herself* said; and he gained an entirely new perspective on the importance of *what* she said, quite apart from her treatment of Oxford Group ideas.

A.A. appears, in its later years, consciously to have distanced and disassociated itself from its Oxford Group roots.[3] So much so, in fact, that the A.A. fellowship seems to speak far more about what A.A. learned *not* to do from, and the supposed reasons it split *with*, the Oxford Group, than to spell out the basic ideas it took *from* the Oxford Group.[4] Thus the characterizations by some of Anne's spiritual research and notes as an "Oxford Group" product may have done much to divert attention from the

---

[3] See *Pass It On* (New York: Alcoholics Anonymous World Services, 1984), pp. 171-74.

[4] See Kurtz, *Not-God*, pp. 50-51, 80-81; *Alcoholics Anonymous Comes of Age* (New York: Alcoholics Anonymous World Services, Inc., 1957), pp. 74-75.

importance of the journal as an almost certain, major source of the spiritual ideas A.A. did adopt for its program of recovery. Perhaps reflecting such thinking, two authors recently, in effect, labeled Anne as a Bible-toting, flag-waving simp.[5] So it seemed more than timely to revisit Anne Smith and the spiritual notes she took and taught to AAs and their families for almost six years before A.A.'s basic text and Twelve Steps were published in 1939.

The results of our new analysis were very exciting. We could and can see that, whether or not originating from Oxford Group influences, A.A. principles, practices, and language fairly leap out of Anne Smith's notes. And, with that, we now return to a revised account of what we set forth at the beginning of our first edition. This to be followed by a completely new and thorough look at Anne Smith's own words about A.A., its Big Book, and Twelve Step ideas.

Anne Ripley Smith, Wife of A.A. Co-founder, Dr. Bob

There was a lady in Akron, Ohio, who had great faith—faith in God, His Word, and the teachings of Jesus Christ. She had faith that God was able and willing to heal her husband and that His Word meant what it said in promising deliverance to those who believe. She believed Jesus Christ was the Way. And she had courage—persisting in her believing despite many, many years of frustration over her husband's seemingly hopeless drinking problem. Most important, she had love—the greatest of the three virtues (faith, courage, and love). Love—which her husband's favorite Bible chapter—1 Corinthians 13—promised her "never

[5] In a recent play, two distinguished authors wrote as to a meeting between Anne and her husband, Dr. Bob: "ANNE enters. A short, solid, no-nonsense woman of fifty-four, she wears dress and hat, and carries a Bible and a small American flag." See Samuel Shem and Janet Surrey, *Bill W. and Dr. Bob* (New York: Samuel French, Inc., 1987), p. 35.

faileth." To those she helped, the lady frequently quoted from 1 John 4:8:

> He that loveth not knoweth not God; for God is love.

The lady gave her love to God, to her husband and two children, and to countless numbers of alcoholics and their families whom she helped. For years, said her husband's biography, she "did what she could to hold the family together and prayed that her husband would somehow find an answer to his problem." Later, her husband himself reflected, "How my wife kept her faith and courage during all those years, I'll never know. . . . If she had not, I know I would have been dead a long time ago."

This lady was Anne Ripley Smith.[6] She was married to an Akron physician, Dr. Robert Holbrook Smith. The Akron physician was an alcoholic.[7] He became the co-founder of Alcoholics Anonymous on June 10, 1935—the day he had his last drink. And the members of Alcoholics Anonymous affectionately called him "Dr. Bob."

In 1933, Anne succeeded in interesting her husband in the Oxford Group—a spiritual movement that sought to recapture the power of First-Century Christianity in the modern world. For the next two-and-a-half years, Dr. Bob studied the Bible, prayed, did extensive spiritual reading, and endeavored to follow Oxford Group practices and principles. Dr. Bob and Anne joined a church, the Westminster Presbyterian Church in Akron, Ohio, following a suggestion of their Oxford Group friends. But Dr. Bob stayed drunk. His wife and their friends were not idle during that period,

---

[6] Many of the facts in this introductory chapter, including two quotes of Dr. Bob, were taken from *DR. BOB and the Good Oldtimers* (New York: Alcoholics Anonymous World Services, Inc., 1980). And more recently, in part, from Smith and Windows, *Children of the Healer*.

[7] See Dr. Bob's story at pages 171-81 of *Alcoholics Anonymous*. 3d ed. (New York: Alcoholics Anonymous World Services, Inc., 1976). Unless otherwise indicated, all further references to this work will be to the popular and affectionate name AAs use for their basic text, namely, the "Big Book."

however. They met, prayed, and studied with Dr. Bob. And on Mother's Day of 1935, their prayers were answered.

Bill Wilson—a sober, but self-styled "rum hound from New York"—arrived in Akron on what became an unsuccessful business deal. Bill was broke and despondent. He had the choice of a drink or a "drunk"—the choice of resuming his alcoholic drinking or working with another alcoholic. He chose the latter. Bill had been sober for six months, after years of drinking. He was a member of the Oxford Group in New York, and had learned he must carry to another alcoholic the message about his dire disease, his spiritual solution, and the Oxford Group's life-changing recovery program. And he followed the suggestion in Akron.

Oxford Group people, and many AAs, firmly believe that Bill was guided by God to make a series of phone calls that kept him from the Mayflower Hotel bar and put him in touch with Akron Oxford Group adherent, Henrietta Seiberling, and very shortly with Dr. Bob himself. Bill W. and Dr. Bob soon became fast friends and co-founders of an A.A. fellowship that today, some sixty-three years later, numbers almost two million members. The rest is well documented A.A. history. The rest, that is, except for the specifics as to what Bill, Dr. Bob, and Anne shared together over the period of three months, in the summer of 1935, when Bill lived with the Smiths in their Akron home—the time when the formative ideas for an A.A. recovery program were actually developed.

From 1935 to 1939, the two recovered alcoholics—Bill W. and Dr. Bob—labored together to help other alcoholics get well. Ere long in this early period, Dr. Bob had achieved substantial success in Akron. A group of some forty alcoholics, most of them in the Akron-Cleveland area, had attained substantial sobriety. Finally, these recovered alcoholics, then numbering perhaps a hundred, determined to publish a book—the Big Book—which they called *Alcoholics Anonymous*. It described what they had done to achieve recovery; and it described twelve spiritual steps they had taken to establish a relationship with God, obtain release from their obsession to drink, and acquire a spiritual design for living.[8] That design, when followed, seemed to restore them to sanity as to their drinking, relieve them of their alcoholism, and provide them with a new deliverance and peace of mind.

Our story concerns what the lady of faith, courage, and love wrote, in the earliest days of A.A., that may have had much to do with the A.A. tenets and practices that have blessed so many alcoholics and their families.

Most of the facts about Anne Smith's journal have been unreported and are virtually unknown to anyone today. Dr. Bob said A.A. got its basic ideas from a study of the Bible, but little had been written as to what those ideas were.[9] Bill W. said A.A.'s spiritual principles came from the Oxford Group, of which he and Dr. Bob were members in early days. Later, Bill attributed the principles primarily to an Oxford Group leader, the Reverend Samuel Moor Shoemaker, Jr., Rector of Calvary Episcopal Church in New York City. But neither Dr. Bob nor Bill spelled out the information and ideas they obtained from the A.A. sources they specified—the Bible, the Oxford Group, or Sam Shoemaker.

In the past three or four years, a number of researchers—the author among them—have examined A.A.'s Biblical, Oxford Group, Shoemaker, and other spiritual sources to identify A.A. ideas at their point of origin. Yet, for a great many years in A.A. Archives in New York (with a copy at Bill Wilson's home in Bedford Hills, New York), there has reposed a work by Anne

---

[8] For uses of this "design for living" term and similar ideas, see the title by Bill Wilson's Oxford Group friend, Victor C. Kitchen, *I Was a Pagan* (New York: Harper & Brothers, 1934), p. 167; and Big Book, pp. 15, 28, 81, 228, 380, 462.

[9] See the results of the author's investigation as to these Biblical ideas in Dick B., *Dr. Bob's Library: Books for Twelve-Step Growth*, Revised Paradise ed. (Kihei, HI: Paradise Research Publications, 1998); *The Oxford Group & Alcoholics Anonymous* (Kihei, HI: Paradise Research Publications, 1998); *The Akron Genesis of Alcoholics Anonymous* (Kihei, HI: Paradise Research Publications, 1998); *New Light on Alcoholism: The A.A. Legacy from Sam Shoemaker* (Kihei, HI: Paradise Research Publications, 1998); *The Good Book and The Big Book: A.A.'s Roots in the Bible*, Bridge Builders Ed. (Kihei, HI: Paradise Research Publications, 1997).

Ripley Smith, that may contain many of the answers they seek as to where A.A.'s spiritual ideas originated.

In January of 1933, an Oxford Group team, headed by Oxford Group Founder, Dr. Frank N. D. Buchman, came to Akron at the behest of rubber magnate Harvey Firestone. Firestone was grateful for what the Oxford Group had done for his alcoholic son, Bud. Bud had gone to an Oxford Group meeting in Denver with Oxford Group activist James Newton. Newton put Bud in touch with the Reverend Sam Shoemaker; and Shoemaker helped Bud Firestone to a religious experience that freed him from the obsession to drink, at least for a time. Thus Harvey Firestone's gratitude.

Upon the senior Firestone's invitation, about thirty Oxford Group "team" members came to Akron and held ten days of meetings. These evangelists filled many Protestant pulpits in the Akron area. The events made headlines. In attendance were Henrietta Seiberling, Anne Ripley Smith, and their friends Clarace Williams and Delphine Weber. Shortly, a Wednesday night Oxford Group meeting was being held in Akron at the home of T. Henry and Clarace Williams.

Members prevailed upon Dr. Bob to attend. This he did for the next two-and-a-half years. He began an intense study of the Bible and did an immense amount of spiritual reading the Oxford Group people recommended. Dr. Bob and Anne observed morning Quiet Time, an Oxford Group practice, and engaged in Bible study, prayer, and listening for God's guidance. They used daily Bible devotionals in their meditations. Prayer assumed large proportions in the Smith family. But the important thing for our purposes is that Anne Smith began assembling what we now call "Anne Smith's Journal."[10] We previously called it her "Spiritual Workbook" because it comprehended much more than just Oxford Group practices and principles, and discussed a host of Bible verses, Biblical principles, and religious writings of her day.

---

[10] Except as hereinafter specifically noted, we shall call Anne Smith's spiritual journal, which was compiled between 1933 and 1939, her "Journal."

Anne Smith's daughter, Sue Smith Windows, wrote the author that Anne compiled her spiritual journal over the period from 1933 to 1939.[11] Sue typed up much of this journal for her mother sometime in 1937-1938 while Sue was attending business college. Copies of the journal wound up in New York. One at Bill W.'s home at Stepping Stones in Bedford Hills where the author was permitted to inspect it. And the other at A.A. General Services Archives in New York. At one point, the document was sent to Sue Smith Windows, but Sue believes a substantial portion was, by that time, missing from the original manuscript she typed and helped her mother index.[12]

At any rate, in 1991, Sue Smith Windows authorized and requested A.A. Archives to provide, to the author of this book and to her, a copy of Anne Smith's spiritual journal; and A.A. General Services cooperated fully. The author scrutinized the notebook with care in light of his research into the spiritual principles that the Oxford Group, Dr. Sam Shoemaker, and Dr. Bob advocated. The author's general study and research are still in progress, but this shorter book is one result.

We believe with others, including Anne's daughter, that Anne's notes show how Anne faithfully studied, organized, and recorded the materials she and Dr. Bob had been reading, listening to at the Oxford Group meetings, discussing with their friend, Henrietta Seiberling, and studying in the Bible, the daily devotionals, and the other spiritual literature that passed their way in the 1930's.[13] The author has read no A.A. history, Conference-approved or otherwise, that suggests or confirms that Bill Wilson read Anne Smith's Journal. Sue Smith Windows could not even be sure her father, Dr. Bob, had read it; but she did affirm that her father had read all the books Anne mentioned and recommended in her journal. It therefore seems highly likely that Anne Smith and

---

[11] Letter from Sue Smith Windows to the author, August 9, 1991.

[12] See Smith and Windows, *Children of the Healer*, p. 29.

[13] See comments in Smith and Windows, *Children of the Healer*, pp. 29, 41, 84, 132; Darrah, *Sister Ignatia*, pp. 115-16.

Henrietta Seiberling—clear of mind and very much enthused over the Bible and Oxford Group principles—passed on to Dr. Bob and to Bill, in the three months that all spent together in the summer of 1935, the spiritual information Anne had compiled and was then compiling.

Our view has now been much reinforced by the eye-witness testimony of John R., an Akron-A.A. oldtimer, who died in 1989. Referring to the meetings early AAs held in Dr. Bob's home to establish and maintain a strong spiritual life, John said:

> Before one of these meetings [in Dr. Bob's home], Anne used to pull out a little book [her spiritual journal] and quote from it. We would discuss it. Then we would see what Anne would suggest from it for our discussion.[14]

Sue windows told the author that AAs used to describe their visits to the Smith home as trips to get their "spiritual pablum."[15]

We know several things for sure about Anne Ripley Smith and early A.A.:

1. From 1933 to 1935, Anne and Dr. Bob attended Akron Oxford Group meetings together at the West Hill Group on Thursdays and later at the T. Henry and Clarace Williams's home on Wednesdays.[16]
2. During the summer of 1935, Anne, Dr. Bob, and Bill W. attended the Wednesday meetings together for the three months that Bill lived with the Smiths.[17]
3. Anne, Dr. Bob, and Bill observed morning Quiet Time together daily in the summer of 1935, when Anne read and interpreted Scripture and other spiritual material.[18]

---

[14] See discussion and documentation in Dick B., *The Akron Genesis*, pp. 109-10.

[15] Dick B., *The Akron Genesis*, p. 110.

[16] *DR. BOB*, pp. 53-58.

[17] *DR. BOB*, pp. 100; *Pass It On*, pp. 145-47.

[18] Kurtz, *Not-God*, p. 32; *Pass It On*, p. 147; *DR. BOB*, pp. 71-72.

4. Anne, Dr. Bob, and Bill had a good many spiritual discussions with Henrietta Seiberling during this period; and Henrietta was the one who "called the shots" at Oxford Group meetings.[19]
5. Dr. Bob and Bill had long discussions of their ideas each night for the three summer months of 1935.[20]
6. Anne had extended discussions with Bill during that period, even when Dr. Bob was not present.[21]
7. Anne faithfully attended meetings of the Oxford Group in the period from 1935 to 1939 before the Big Book was published—meetings in which the alcoholics termed themselves the "alcoholic squad of the Oxford Group."[22]
8. Anne regularly attended meetings after they moved from the Williams home to King's School and became A.A.'s King School Group, Akron Number One.[23]
9. Anne worked individually with many alcoholics and with their wives in the Smith home.[24]
10. Bill Wilson called Anne Ripley Smith the "Mother of A.A." And he asked her to write the chapter of the Big Book, titled "To Wives" (though Anne declined).[25]

---

[19] *DR. BOB*, pp. 53-60, 157; Sue Smith Windows, *Henrietta and early Oxford Group Friends* (typewritten memorandum provided to the author by Sue Smith Windows at Akron Ohio in June, 1991); Kurtz, *Not-God*, p. 40; *The Language of the Heart* (New York: The A.A. Grapevine, Inc., 1988), p. 357.

[20] *DR. BOB*, p. 97.

[21] Telephone interview of Sue Smith Windows by the author in December, 1991.

[22] *DR. BOB*. pp. 87-88, 219, 137, 128, 100; Personal interview of the author with Sue Smith Windows in Akron in June, 1991.

[23] *DR. BOB*, p. 106.

[24] *DR. BOB* 114-17.

[25] See *DR. BOB*, p. 152; Smith and Windows, *Children of the Healer*, pp. 29, 43, 132; *The Language of the Heart*, p. 353. Sue Smith Windows wrote the author on August 10, 1991, that Bill referred to Anne Smith as the "Mother of A.A." In a telephone call to the author in early 1992, Eddie S., an oldtimer from Colorado, who knew Bill and Lois Wilson and Dr. Bob and Anne quite well, confirmed that she had heard Bill Wilson speak of Anne as the "Mother of A.A."

None of the foregoing facts proves that Bill Wilson read or heard or even was aware of Anne Smith's Journal. But the facts do establish convincingly that Anne Smith was very much a part of the prayer, Bible study, Quiet Times, spiritual thinking, Oxford Group meetings, and lengthy discussions of the Oxford Group program and of spiritual ideas, that took place in the Smith home in the summer of 1935 and every year thereafter until her death.

Bill and Bob and Anne were living together. They were broke. None—not even Dr. Bob—had a job demanding significant outside time. Their focus—individually and collectively—was on sobriety, a spiritual solution, and helping alcoholics to recover.

So, we here review Anne Smith's Journal as probably the only detailed, extant record of just what was probably under discussion in the Akron, Ohio, home of Dr. and Mrs. Smith in the summer of 1935.[26] We cannot be sure that Bill, Dr. Bob, and Anne sat down together and discussed each item. But all three were at work to the same end. Anne was the lady—clear of mind and patient of purpose—who provided the faith, courage, spiritual infusions, and love that supported Dr. Bob and Bill in their new-found Biblically-oriented, Oxford Group partnership of service to other alcoholics. Dr. Bob and Bill—fervent in their Oxford Group spiritual approach—were tearing around the Akron area "oxidizing" drunks.[27] We shall see from Anne Smith's Journal that she had the "oxidant" down in writing. And in our next chapter we shall review Anne's own words and compare them with words found in A.A. and which tend to show Anne's immense influence on the thinking and writing of Bill Wilson as he put together A.A.'s program of recovery in A.A.'s Big Book and Twelve Steps.

---

[26] See Sue Smith Windows's recollections as to the extended discussions Bill Wilson and Dr. Bob, and Bill Wilson and Anne Smith would have each day in the summer of 1935, often until 2:00 in the morning. *Children of the Healer*, p. 39.

[27] *DR. BOB*, p. 78.

What They Said about Anne

Before we commence our review of Anne's notes, we'll set forth here a few of the many comments about Anne that show the lady's heart. Dr. Bob's son and daughter-in-law provided the author with many of the letters which people wrote to Bill Wilson and others at the time of Anne's death and which spoke to Anne's personal characteristics, spiritual depth, and immense contributions to A.A. But apparently Wilson never completed or caused to be published in A.A.'s *Grapevine* the article that was supposed to have told the details about Anne's role.[28]

The following are, however, just a few of many remarks about her:

> [Bill Wilson:] With those who knew her not, I wish to share the inspiration which she gave to Lois [Lois Wilson] and me. Anne was the wife of Dr. Bob, co-founder of Alcoholics Anonymous. She was, quite literally, the mother of our first group, Akron Number One. Her wise and beautiful counsel to all, her insistence that the spiritual come before anything else, her unwavering support of Dr. Bob in all his works; all these were virtues which watered the uncertain seed that was to become AA. Who but God could assess such a contribution? We can only say that it was priceless and magnificent. In the full sense of the word, she was one of the founders of Alcoholics Anonymous.[29]

> [Bill Wilson:] For the next three months I lived with these two wonderful people [Dr. Bob and Anne]. I shall always believe they gave me more than I ever brought them. . . . Then [after the first few weeks] came a lull on the Twelfth Step front. In this time Anne and Henrietta [Seiberling] infused much needed spirituality into Bob and me. . . . The devotion of this good man [Dr. Bob]

---

[28] Smith and Windows, *Children of the Healer*, p. 84.

[29] *The Language of the Heart*, pp. 353-54.

and his wife is a bright page in memory. Their names will be inscribed on page one of AA's book of first and best friends.[30]

[Bill Wilson:] Bob and Anne and Henrietta [Seiberling] have been working so hard with those men and with really wonderful success. . . . Anne and Bob and Henrietta have done a great job.[31]

[Bill Wilson:] . . . Clevelanders had gone to Dr. Bob's Akron home, sitting with him and Anne over cups of coffee at their kitchen table. Eagerly they had absorbed knowledge of their problem and its solution and had breathed deeply of the remarkable spiritual atmosphere of the place.[32]

[Lois Wilson:] I loved Annie and Bob from the moment I saw them. They were so warm, so gracious, so *good*. . . . As Annie, a most loving and understanding person, had weak eyes, she used to sit in a dark corner of the living room, smoking endless cigarettes. Soon Annie was showing great wisdom in giving help and advice to those who sought it. In the years to come, that little, dark corner of 855 Ardmore Avenue [in Akron, Ohio] became a haven for those in trouble, both alcoholics and their families.[33]

[Lois Wilson:] Annie had belonged to the Oxford Group before we [Bill and Lois Wilson] met her and had felt the need for her own spiritual growth, as I did. . . . So whenever we met with the wives of other AAs, we each told them how we had come to the decision to live by the same principles as our mates and how we were now endeavoring to follow these principles. . . . Annie's part in the formation of AA and consequently in the foundation of Al-Anon should never be forgotten, especially by Family Group members. Although there were few Family Groups during the thirteen years of her activity, Annie did much to instill the spirit of

---

[30] *The Language of the Heart*, pp. 356-57.

[31] Bill Wilson writing to his wife, Lois, from Akron. See *DR. BOB*, p. 108.

[32] *Alcoholics Anonymous Comes of Age*, p. 19.

[33] *Lois Remembers* (New York: Al-Anon Family Group Headquarters, 1991), p. 96.

Al-Anon in many of the families of alcoholics. God bless Annie's memory.[34]

[*DR. BOB* reported:] Annie Smith never stopped showing her love and concern for others in this way. Another woman, Peggy, recalled that in the year before Anne died, "there was seldom a morning when she didn't call."[35]

[Dorothy S. M.:] I walked in there [to an early A.A. meeting], and all these people came up to me. One of the very first was Anne Smith. Somebody introduced her to me as Mrs. Smith, and she said, "Call me Annie." Well, that did it. I could hardly even talk. It seemed to break the shell that I had been so careful to build up all those years.[36]

[Dorothy S. M.:] Anne had a "deep sense of believing in her guidance . . ."[37]

[Dorothy S. M.:] They [Dr. Bob and Anne] loved everybody, and their home was just full of people. It was like Grand Central Station. They'd come up to our house to get away from the tremendous pressure—people dropping in on them all the time. I always felt privileged.[38]

[Arch T.:] I had been taken in off the streets and nursed back to life by Anne Smith. I was not only penniless and jobless, but too ill to get out of the house during the day and hunt for work. So great was Anne's love and so endless her patience with me, so understanding her handling of me, that ten months later, I left a new man, perhaps imbued with just a few grains of that love. Their love for each other and for their two children was of such a nature that it permeated the house, and if one lived in that house

---

[34] *Lois Remembers*, pp. 172-73.

[35] *DR. BOB*, p. 87.

[36] Dorothy S. M., (wife of early A.A. Clarence S.), *DR. BOB*, p. 145.

[37] *DR. BOB*, p. 115.

[38] *DR. BOB*, p. 278.

and were willing, that same love was bound to get under one's skin.[39]

He [Arch T.] gave credit for this change of heart to Anne Smith, and cited it as another example of her wise understanding and patience, since she always waited for Archie "to search out the answers for myself . . . and then for me to pursue the path that these answers indicated."[40]

[Bob E.:] She had a quiet, soft way of making you feel at home. I shared a good many of my life problems with her. She read the Bible and counseled with me. She tried to keep things simple, too. I told her about being nervous and demoralized. She gave me a couple of phrases to say whenever I got downhearted or confused or frustrated. One I remember is: "God is love."[41] And I used it consistently.[42]

[Annabelle G.:] Then Anne Smith took me under her wing. She told me a lot and called me up every day. I saw Wally was taking an interest; he was different. So I decided I would find out what it was all about myself. I started to study, and you know, it has done me every bit as much good as it has done Wally.[43]

[Dan K.:] Anne always looked to the newcomers. . . . She'd spot you, and after the meeting, she would go to your table and introduce herself. "I want to welcome you and your lovely wife to Alcoholics Anonymous. We hope you'll keep coming back." She'd give a little bit of background on A.A. and then maybe she'd go to another new member.[44]

---

[39] Arch T., who carried the message to Detroit, in *DR. BOB*, p. 115.

[40] *DR. BOB*, p. 182.

[41] See 1 John 4:8, 16.

[42] Bob E., an early Akron AA, in *DR. BOB*, pp. 116-17.

[43] Annabelle G., wife of A.A. oldtimer, Wally G., in *DR. BOB*, p. 121.

[44] Dan K. in *DR. BOB*, p. 233.

> Anne's concern for the newcomer was both legendary and phenomenal—a greater concern, perhaps, than that of most A.A. members.[45]
>
> [Elgie R.:] Doc used to shake his head and say, "Well, I think I'd better work with the men, because the women . . . I'm not sure. I don't know." And Annie would say, "Let's try and see." She always felt if you don't try, you never know.[46]
>
> [Duke:] Anne gave us a feeling of stability. . . . She always had the right thing to say, no matter what. You couldn't have a feeling of anger or animosity toward anyone when she was around. She always said, in order to know someone's feelings you had to walk a mile in his shoes.[47]
>
> [Bob S., Anne's son:] Tolerance did not come easily to Dr. Bob. "I have heard him say it was difficult for him to be tolerant . . . that it was not his nature and a real hurdle. He got it [tolerance] from Mom, and he had to work on it real hard."[48]
>
> [Betty S., Anne's daughter-in-law:] She was a sheltered place for people in trouble. . . . I doubt that any minister in any given week could have counseled more people, prayed with more people. In times of trouble, people rushed to her. She was a rock, a comforter with God's help—truly a person who went placidly amid noise and haste."[49]

As stated, the author is in possession of copies of a large number of letters about Anne Smith that were provided by her son, Bob; and most speak of her loving, unselfish, kind, and thoughtful qualities. Perhaps the most detailed is an eight-page memorandum

---

[45] *DR. BOB*, p. 233.

[46] Elgie R., an Akron oldtimer, explaining how the barrier against helping women alcoholics was broken down through Anne's help. See *DR. BOB*, p. 242.

[47] *DR. BOB*, p. 255.

[48] *DR. BOB*, p. 272.

[49] Betty S., Anne's daughter-in-law, in *DR. BOB*, p. 304.

by Florence B. of Akron, dated January 19, 1950. It described Anne's A.A. contributions in detail and told of friends moving in and out of her house at will and of her helping new AAs to find jobs. Florence called Anne: "evangelist, nurse, salesman, employment bureau, all in one." She concluded, as to Anne's religious convictions:

> Anne's personal religion was simple and workable. She never sought to rewrite the Bible nor to explain it. She just accepted it.[50]

And now to just what it was that Anne was sharing with the thousands who came to her for solace, inspiration, and counsel.

---

[50] See Dick B., *The Akron Genesis*, pp. 108-09. While this tribute is generous and probably correctly implies that Anne did not quarrel with the Bible as containing the will of God, it does not portray the depth of Anne's *belief* in the Bible. Anne studied it, analyzed it, quoted it, shared it, explained it, and tried to live by it—as we shall show.

2

The Elements of the Twelve Steps

Anne Smith began a spiritual quest, and also began keeping her spiritual Journal, in 1933. Her daughter, Sue, recalls that year as the starting point. And Anne frequently referred in her Journal to an Oxford Group Houseparty of 1933. We cannot be sure that Anne was referring specifically to the famous visit of Oxford Group Founder, Dr. Frank Buchman, and his team of thirty, to Akron, Ohio, in January, 1933. However, she must at least have been referring to Oxford Group activities which began in Akron at that time. The Akron newspaper articles in January, 1933, told of Oxford Group events that centered around the Firestone family, the deliverance of Russell ("Bud") Firestone from alcoholism, and team witnessing in churches and at the Mayflower Hotel. But the papers also spoke of plans for subsequent houseparties and continuance of the Oxford Group team's work. History records that Anne Smith, T. Henry and Clarace Williams, Delphine Weber, and Henrietta Seiberling began attending Oxford Group events almost at once; and they were soon followed by Dr. Bob.

What is striking about Anne's spiritual Journal is its very specific language pertaining to, and its precise formulation of, each of twelve concepts Bill Wilson later codified into A.A.'s Twelve Steps for recovery from alcoholism. Incidentally, Anne scarcely mentions liquor, but she certainly begins at the beginning—with the unmanageable life and the need for turning to God for help.

Here are her ideas as they seem to have found their way into the Twelve Steps, as AAs later put them together in 1939.

The Unmanageable Life and Step One

At three different places in her Journal, Anne prescribed a prayer for beginning one's search for a relationship with God. She wrote:

> *What do you do when you pray? O Lord manage me, for I cannot manage myself.* That we are so in touch with the Holy Spirit that he can give us at that moment a message that is accurate and adequate. That is the release you want with people. Your prayers should always be different and straight to the point (pp. 26, 51, italics added).

> Surrender is a simple act of will. What do we surrender? Our life. When? At a certain definite moment. How? *Oh God, manage me because I cannot manage myself* (p. 42, italics added).

Anne did not specify her source for this prayer. But the prayer was common in Oxford Group and Sam Shoemaker circles.

In his well-known Oxford Group book, *For Sinners Only*, A. J. Russell described the prayer from Dr. Frank Buchman's story about "Victor," and how Victor surrendered and had his life changed. Recounting at great length how Buchman converted Victor at a schoolboys' camp in the Himalayas, Russell recounted the following conversation between Buchman and Victor:

> [Buchman said:] What we need is faith. When we are perfectly willing to forsake sin and follow Christ, then joy and release come. What we want to do is to get in touch with Him and turn our lives over to Him. Where should we go to do it? At once the lad replied: "There is only one place—on our knees." The lad prayed—one of those powerful, simple prayers which are so

> quickly heard by Him Who made the eye and the ear: "*O Lord, manage me, for I cannot manage myself*" (italics added).[1]

Variations of this "Victor story" and prayer were told again and again in Oxford Group writings.[2]

Shoemaker described a similar surrender procedure and prayer. His church called the prayer "Charlie's Prayer." Shoemaker's long-time associate and assistant minister gave this account:

> One morning, as the two [Shoemaker and a poorly educated "east-sider" named Charlie] chatted in the rectory hallway, "it" happened. No one knows what the rector said on that occasion, but new life came to Charlie, and those who heard about Charlie's prayer could never forget it. It was a classic, a simple plea in eight words: "*God, manage me, 'cause I can't manage myself*" (italics added).[3]

The Big Book's First Step language reads as follows:

> We admitted we were powerless over alcohol—that *our lives had become unmanageable* (p. 59, italics added).

And this is followed by A.A.'s well-known "a,b,c's," which are set forth as follows in its Big Book:

> Our description of the alcoholic, the chapter to the agnostic, and our personal adventures before and after make clear three pertinent

---

[1] See A. J. Russell, *For Sinners Only* (London: Hodder & Stoughton, 1932), p. 79.

[2] See Peter Howard, *Frank Buchman's Secret* (New York: Doubleday & Co., 1961), pp. 41-44; Theophil Spoerri, *Dynamic out of Silence: Frank Buchman's Relevance Today* (London: Grosvenor Books, 1976), pp. 34-37; Garth Lean, *On the Tail of a Comet: The Life of Frank Buchman* (Colorado Springs; Helmers & Howard, 1988), pp. 112-13; and Cecil Rose, *When Man Listens* (New York: Oxford University Press, 1937), pp. 19-22.

[3] See Irving Harris, *The Breeze of the Spirit: Sam Shoemaker and the Story of Faith-at-Work* (New York: The Seabury Press, 1978), p. 10. See also Samuel M. Shoemaker, *How to Find God*. Reprint from Faith at Work Magazine, n.d., p. 6; *How You Can Help Other People* (New York: E. P. Dutton & Co., 1946), p. 60.

> ideas: (a) That we were alcoholic *and could not manage our own lives*. (b) That probably no human power could have relieved our alcoholism. (c) That God could and would if He were sought (p. 60, italics added).

A Power Greater Than Ourselves and Step Two

Anne's language about "a power stronger than ourselves" closely resembles Big Book language. In a portion of her Journal which is titled, "Introduction," she spoke of this power. Her discussion had to do with "the beginning of the discovery that we can be set free from sin." Anne mentioned Romans 8, and the Apostle Paul, and said:

> Paul speaks of a wish toward good, but power to carry it out is lacking. *A stronger power than his was needed*. God provided the power through Christ, so that we could find a new kind of relationship with God. Christ gives the power, we appropriate it. It is not anything that we do ourselves; but it is the appropriation of a power that comes from God that saves us from sin and sets us free (p. 37, italics added).

Anne repeated this language at page 56 of her Journal. The concept of a Power greater than one's own self, as a solution, was much discussed in Oxford Group literature mentioned by Anne and read by others in the Akron area. For example, in his chapter, titled "The Solution," the popular Oxford Group writer, Stephen Foot, devoted a page to the solution, and stated:

> There is at work in the world to-day a Power that has for many generations been neglected by masses of mankind, a Power that can change human nature—that is the message of this book. It is like the great power of the Niagara Falls, which existed for millenniums before man inhabited the earth. Then for thousands of years man lacked the knowledge to use the power and so it ran to waste. To-day, harnessed, it is bringing light into thousands of homes. So with this Power by which human nature can be

> changed. I have felt it in my own life and seen it at work in the lives of others; it is at work all over the world to-day, and through this Power problems are being solved.[4]

In one of the first popular Oxford Group books, Harold Begbie wrote:

> The future of civilization, rising at this moment from the ruins of materialism, would seem to lie in an intelligent use by man of this ultimate source of spiritual Power.[5]

In the Big Book chapter, "There is a Solution," Bill Wilson makes clear that will-power alone will not solve problems (pp. 22, 44). He points to the solution: establishing a relationship with God (p. 29). Then in his chapter, "We Agnostics," Bill wrote:

> Lack of power, that was our dilemma. We had to find a power by which we could live, and it had to be a *Power greater than ourselves*. Obviously. But where and how were we to find this Power? Well, that's exactly what this book is about. Its main object is to enable you to find a Power greater than yourself which will solve your problem. . . . And it means, of course, that we are going to talk about God (p. 45).

> We found that as soon as we were able to lay aside prejudice and express even a willingness to believe in a *Power greater than ourselves*, we commenced to get results, even though it was impossible for any of us to fully define or comprehend that *Power, which is God* (p. 46, italics added).

A.A.'s Big Book not only states specifically, but also makes clear by the frequency of its mention, that the aim of its recovery program is the establishment of a relationship with God.[6]

---

[4] Stephen Foot, *Life Began Yesterday* (New York: Harper & Brothers, 1935), p. 22.

[5] Harold Begbie, *Life Changers* (London: Mills & Boon, 1932), p. 22.

[6] See Big Book, pp. 29, 13, 28, 100, 164.

Shoemaker spoke of this relationship with similar frequency.[7] Thus in *Children of the Second Birth*, he wrote:

> We believe entirely that conversion is the experience which initiates the new life. But we are not fools enough to think that the beginning is the end! All subsequent life is a development of the relationship with God which conversion opened (p. 16).

Anne wrote:

> We must be in such relationship with God that He *can* guide us (p. 8, italics in original).
>
> God provided the power through Christ, so that we could find a new kind of relationship with God (p. 37).
>
> 2nd step. To get in right relationship with God (p. 62).
>
> Takes whole power of Christ to help us do the smallest thing. Step that puts man in position to receive the grace of God who alone commands. Surrender sins and wills putting God's will ahead. Whole thing begins to work (p. 57).

The Decision to Surrender to God As You Understand Him and Step Three

A.A., Oxford Group, and Shoemaker language all emphasize that the path to a relationship with God via a spiritual experience begins with a *decision* to surrender to God. Anne's treatment of the subject was no less precise. Our own discussion of the surrender topic must be divided into three parts: (1) The decision. (2) God *as you understand Him*. (3) The surrender itself.

---

[7] Samuel M. Shoemaker, *Realizing Religion* (New York: Association Press, 1923), p. 42; *Confident Faith* (New York: Fleming H. Revell, 1932), p. 110; *Christ's Words from the Cross* (New York: Fleming H. Revell, 1933), p. 49; *National Awakening* (New York: Harper & Brothers, 1936), p. 13.

1. *The decision.*

Speaking of a *decision* and "God *as you understand Him,*" Anne wrote:

> Try to bring a person to a *decision* to "surrender as much of himself as he knows to as much of God as he knows." Stay with him until he makes a *decision* and says it aloud (p. 4, italics added).

Oxford Group people also stated one must make a *decision* to surrender. One basic primer, *What Is The Oxford Group?*, said:

> The Oxford Group initial act of Surrender is not, in any way, an outward and visible ceremony we feel we must shrink from; it is a simple decision put into simple language, spoken aloud to God, in front of a witness, at any time in any place, that we have decided to forget the past in God and to give our future into His keeping. Nothing more need be added; . . .[8]

Embodying this *decision* in A.A.'s Step Three, the Big Book said:

> Made a decision to turn our will and our lives over to the care of God *as we understood Him* (p. 59, italics in original).
>
> Being convinced, *we were at Step Three*, which is that we decided to turn our will and our life over to God as we understood Him (p. 60, italics in original).

---

[8] The Layman with a Notebook, *What Is The Oxford Group?* (London: Oxford University Press, 1933), p. 47. See also Henry B. Wright, *The Will of God and a Man's Lifework* (New York: Young Men's Christian Association Press, 1909), pp. 43-114; Ebenezer Macmillan, *Seeking and Finding* (New York: Harper & Brothers, 1933), p. 273; Samuel M. Shoemaker, *Children of the Second Birth* (New York: Fleming H. Revell, 1927), pp. 175-87; *Religion That Works* (New York: Fleming H. Revell, 1928), pp. 46-47; *If I Be Lifted Up* (New York: Fleming H. Revell, 1931), p. 93; *The Conversion of the Church* (New York: Fleming H. Revell, 1932), pp. 39-40, 77; *The Church Can Save the World* (New York: Harper & Brothers, 1938), p. 120.

> This is the how and why of it. First of all, we had to quit playing God. It didn't work. Next, we decided that hereafter in this drama of life, God was going to be our Director (p. 62).

> Though our decision was a vital and crucial step, it could have little permanent effect unless at once followed by a strenuous effort to face, and to be rid of, the things in ourselves which had been blocking us (p. 64).

2. *God as you understand Him.*

A.A. legend has it that a former atheist, Jim B., authored the A.A. concept of "God as we understand Him" as it is expressed in A.A.'s Twelve Steps.[9] Bill Wilson acknowledged there had been a controversy over use of the word "God" in the Twelve Steps, but we are not aware that Bill himself ever affirmed Jim B.'s claim that he (Jim) was the author of God *as we understand Him*.[10] In fact, in two different early accounts of his first visits with his friend and sponsor, Ebby Thacher, Bill indicated that Ebby himself had suggested to Bill in 1934 that Bill should surrender himself to God *as Bill understood Him*.[11] Furthermore,

---

[9] See, for example, Jim B.'s own statement of his claim in his Big Book story at page 248. Jim B. made the same claim on page 5 of a document he wrote, titled *Evolution of Alcoholics Anonymous*. A copy was supplied to the author by Eddie S., an oldtimer from Colorado.

[10] See, for example, Bill's account in *Alcoholics Anonymous Comes of Age* (New York: Alcoholics Anonymous World Services, 1957), pp. 17, 166-67; and Ruth Hock's account in *Pass It On* (New York: Alcoholics Anonymous World Services, 1984), p. 199.

[11] See Bill Wilson, *Original Story*, a thirty-four page document located at the archives at Bill's Home at Stepping Stones. Each line of the document is numbered; and the author was given a copy. On page 30, Bill stated: "This is what my friend [Ebby Thacher] suggested I do: Turn my face to God as I understand Him and say to Him with earnestness—complete honesty and abandon—that I henceforth place my life at His disposal and Direction forever" (lines 989-92). See also W. W., "The Fellowship of Alcoholics Anonymous," *Quarterly Journal of Studies on Alcohol* (Yale University, 1945): pp. 461-73, in which Bill is quoted on page 463 as saying that Ebby Thacher told him, "So, call on God as you understand God. Try prayer."

the Oxford Group and Sam Shoemaker had often spoken of "surrendering as much of yourself as you understand to as much of God as you understand."[12] Hence Ebby's suggestion to Bill was quite consistent with what Ebby had heard in the Oxford Group prior to the existence of A.A. Some Oxford Group writers used language quite similar to that which Anne used and which we quoted above. Thus Stephen Foot wrote:

> Life began for me with a surrender of all that I know of self, to all that I knew of God.[13]

> Are you prepared to do His will, let the cost be what it may? That is surrender of all one knows of self to all one knows of God.[14]

3. *The surrender.*

Anne defined surrender by referring to the language Professor William James used in *The Varieties of Religious Experience.*[15] James wrote:

> To be converted, to be regenerated, to receive grace, to experience religion, to gain an assurance, are so many phrases which denote the process, gradual or sudden, by which a self hitherto divided, and consciously wrong, inferior, and unhappy, becomes unified and consciously right, superior, and happy, in consequence of its firmer hold upon religious realities (p. 177).

---

[12] See Samuel M. Shoemaker, *Children of the Second Birth* (New York: Fleming H. Revell, 1927), pp. 27, 47; *How to Become a Christian* (New York: Harper & Brothers, 1953), p. 72; *How to Find God*, p. 6; "In Memoriam" (Princeton, The Graduate Council, June 10, 1956), pp. 2-3. See Dick B., *New Light on Alcoholism: The A.A. Legacy from Sam Shoemaker* (CA: Good Book Publishing Company, 1994), pp. 45, 350.

[13] Foot, *Life Began Yesterday*, pp. 12-13.

[14] Foot, *Life Began Yesterday*, p. 175. See also James D. Newton, *Uncommon Friends* (New York: Harcourt Brace, 1987), p. 154.

[15] William James, *The Varieties of Religious Experience* (New York: Vintage Books, 1990).

Prefacing her use of the foregoing definition, Anne suggested that one surrender as much of himself as he knows to as much of God as he knows. She then wrote:

> Release—surrender—conversion. William James defines it as "that process, gradual or sudden, by which a self divided, inferior, unhappy, and consciously wrong, becomes united, superior, happy, and consciously right." We usually have both sudden and gradual elements in our surrender (pp. 28, 56).

Sam Shoemaker frequently quoted the William James definition.[16] And other Oxford Group writers referred to it.[17] Bill Wilson specifically referred to *The Varieties of Religious Experience* on page 28 of the Big Book, later calling William James one of the "founders" of Alcoholics Anonymous.[18] The William James book was also a favorite of Dr. Bob's.[19]

Writing of surrender, Anne said, "a real 100% surrender" meant surrender of a wide variety of things: (1) Will. (2) Thought of life. (3) Imagination. (4) Sub-conscious mind. (5) Time. (6) Possessions. (7) Possessive relationships. (8) Emotion. (9) Pride. (10) Fears. (11) Self Indulgence. (12) Laziness. (13) Tongue. (14) Plans "and all my rights." (15) Memory (p. 45). Anne used surrender language very similar to that in the Big Book's Third Step discussion, and to that used by Sam Shoemaker. She wrote:

> Surrender is a complete handing over of our wills to God, a reckless abandon of ourselves, all that we have, all that we think,

---

[16] Shoemaker, *Realizing Religion*, p. 30; and see Dick B., *New Light on Alcoholism: The A.A. Legacy from Sam Shoemaker* (CA: Good Book Publishing Co., 1994), p. 41, n. 2.

[17] Compare Harold Begbie, *Twice-Born Men* (New York: Fleming H. Revell, 1909), pp. 16-18; *Life Changers*, p. 126; H. A. Walter, *Soul Surgery*, 6th ed. (Oxford: Printed at the University Press, 1940), p. 80.

[18] *Pass It On*, p. 124.

[19] Dick B., *Dr. Bob's Library*, rev. ed. (CA: Paradise Research Publications, 1994), pp. 51-52.

that we are, everything we hold dear, to God to do what he likes with . . . (p. 42).

Surrender . . . 1st step the life & will. Surrender--fears--sins--most of all their wills--putting God's will ahead of everything (p. 61).

Sam Shoemaker had written:

[Of a parishioner:] She surrendered to God her groundless fears, and with them turned over to Him her life for His direction.[20]

[Quoting a minister he described as "The Militant Mystic":] That night I decided to "launch out into the deep:" and with the decision to cast my will and my life on God, there came an indescribable sense of relief, of burdens dropping away.[21]

The Big Book's "Third Step Prayer" and discussion read:

God, I offer myself to Thee—to build with me and to do with me as Thou wilt. Relieve me of the bondage of self, that I may better do Thy will. Take away my difficulties, that victory over them may bear witness to those I would help of Thy Power, Thy Love, and Thy Way of life. May I do Thy will always! We thought well before taking this step making sure we were ready; that we could at last abandon ourselves utterly to Him (p. 63).

Self-examination, the Moral Inventory and Step Four

Anne framed self-examination in terms of moral values, writing:

Why are people so afraid to face their deepest problems? Because they think there is no answer. When they learn there is one, they

---

[20] Shoemaker, *Children of the Second Birth*, p. 82.

[21] Samuel M. Shoemaker, *Twice-Born Ministers* (New York: Fleming H. Revell, 1929), p. 134.

> will believe it can work out for them, and they will be really honest about themselves. . . . It is absolutely necessary to face people with the moral test. Fundamentally, sin is independence toward God, living without God. Seeing one's self as God sees one, brings hatred out of sin (p. 4).
>
> It's not self-examination but God's examination (p. 44).
>
> Much criticism is second-hand gossip. . . . When people persistently criticize, ask them, "What's wrong with *you*?" Years of clinical experience are back of this principle (p. 3).

Anne cited several Bible verses from the Sermon on the Mount, which were quoted in the Oxford Group and followed in A.A. They emphasized looking for your own fault, your own part in a bad relationship with another human being. Matthew 7:1-5 said:

> Judge not, that ye be not judged. For with what judgment ye judge, ye shall be judged: and with what measure ye mete, it shall be measured to you again. And why beholdest thou the mote [speck] that is in thy brother's eye, but considerest not the beam [log] that is in thine own eye? Or how wilt thou say to thy brother, Let me pull out the mote out of thine eye; and, behold, a beam *is* in thine own eye? Thou hypocrite, first cast out the beam out of thine own eye; and then shalt thou see clearly to cast out the mote out of thy brother's eye.[22]

Anne wrote:

> Who checks another checks himself. If I have an urge to check because of personal feelings, I am not seeing in light of Christ's

---

[22] For Oxford Group writings citing these verses, see Allen, *He That Cometh*, pp. 81, 140; Victor Kitchen, *I Was a Pagan* (New York: Harper & Brothers, 1934), pp. 110-11; Shoemaker, *The Church Can Save the World*, pp. 81-121; *God's Control* (New York: Fleming H. Revell, 1939), pp. 62-72. The verses were also cited in the popular devotional, Oswald Chambers, *My Utmost for His Highest* ((London: Simpkin Marshall, 1927), pp. 169-74; Compare Russell, *For Sinners Only*, pp. 309-16.

> love. Criticism born of my own projection. Something wrong in me. Unless I can crystalize the criticism, *I had better look for mote in my eye* (p. 7, italics added).

A.A.'s Big Book said:

> First, we searched out the flaws in our make-up which caused our failure (p. 64).
>
> Putting out of our minds the wrongs others had done, we resolutely looked for our own mistakes. Where had we been selfish, dishonest, self-seeking and frightened? Though a situation had not been entirely our fault, we tried to disregard the other person involved entirely. Where were we to blame? The inventory was ours, not the other man's (p. 67).
>
> Where had we been selfish, dishonest, or inconsiderate? Whom had we hurt? Did we unjustifiably arouse jealousy, suspicion or bitterness? Where were we at fault . . . (p. 69)?

The Oxford Group stressed the importance of "making the moral test."[23] H. A. Walter's *Soul Surgery* was one of the earliest Oxford Group "texts." Dr. Bob used Walter's book a great deal. And Walter said that the concept, "make the moral test," came from Frank Buchman's and Sherwood Eddy's "Ten Suggestions for Personal Work."[24] Anne specifically mentioned Eddy's ten suggestions in her Journal (p. 14).

The moral test meant examining one's life to see how it measured up to the Oxford Group's Four Absolutes—honesty, purity, unselfishness, and love.[25] It meant writing down on a

---

[23] See Dick B., *The Oxford Group & Alcoholics Anonymous* (Kihei, HI: Paradise Research Publications, 1998), pp. 185-87.

[24] Walter, *Soul Surgery*, pp. 43-44.

[25] See C. Rose, *When Man Listens*, pp. 18-19; Oliver Jones, *Inspired Children* (New York: Harper & Brothers, 1933), pp. 47-68; *Inspired Youth* (New York: Harper & Brothers, 1938), p. 41; Hallen Viney, *How Do I Begin?* (The Oxford Group, 1937), pp. 2-4.

piece of paper the items in a person's life which showed where that person had fallen short of the standards set by Jesus Christ in the Sermon on the Mount and elsewhere. The standards could also be found in other New Testament writings. Sam Shoemaker summarized the self-examination technique as follows:

> It would be a very good thing if you took a piece of foolscap paper and wrote down the sins you feel guilty of. Don't make them up—there will be plenty without that. . . . One of the simplest and best rules for self-examination that I know is to use the Four Standards which Dr. Robert E. Speer said represented the summary of the Sermon on the Mount—Absolute Honesty, Absolute Purity, Absolute Unselfishness, and Absolute Love. Review your life in their light. Put down everything that doesn't measure up. Be ruthlessly, realistically honest.[26]

Anne certainly advocated testing or checking conduct against the four standards of Jesus Christ. She wrote:

> Test your thoughts. It is possible to receive suggestions from your subconscious mind. Check your thoughts by the four standards of Christ (p. 9).
>
> [Quoting from Frank Buchman's ten suggestions for personal work, Anne wrote:] Make the moral test. 4 Standards (p. 14).
>
> Basis of an Interview. Is a challenge on the four standards (p. 29).
>
> What to do with a person who is muddle-headed? Make a list. Help them to make a list of things (pp. 25, 29).
>
> What thoughts do I expect? Am I ready to write them down and willing? It is not making my mind a blank but trusting God to use my mind, my thought life and my imagination. First of all come

---

[26] Shoemaker, *How to Become a Christian*, pp. 56-57. See also Shoemaker, *The Conversion of the Church*, pp. 30-34; *Twice-Born Ministers*, p. 182; *God's Control*, pp. 104-05.

> uncomfortable thoughts of wrong relationships with family, friends and people I work with. Resentments to be faced and set right. Restitution to be made, bills, letters, untidy desks, or house to be set straight (p. 43).
>
> Behind every general need is a particular moral need, so that a general surrender will focus into one point (p. 51).
>
> Surrender on one's moral issue. Destroy the thing that [?] nearest. Then next step becomes plain (p. 57).

Anne also made other references to the four absolutes, or four standards, and stated:

> Why I [?]—had been absolutely honest but not living (p. 7).
>
> [Referring to love:] Follow Christ's absolute commandment (p. 22).
>
> Absolute honesty demands that we no longer wear a mask (p. 32).
>
> Sharing . . . It is being honest even after it hurts (p. 34).
>
> Every time we register aloud the new attitude and change of heart with absolute honesty another bridge is burned behind us and another stake is driven in to anchor and mark our progress (p. 46).
>
> Check your life constantly by the four absolutes (p. 49).

The Four Absolutes had much vitality in early A.A. *DR. BOB and the Good Oldtimers* stated the following:

> At the core of the program were the "four absolutes": absolute honesty, absolute unselfishness, absolute purity, and absolute love.
>
> (In 1948, Dr. Bob recalled the absolutes as "the only yardsticks" Alcoholics Anonymous had in the early days, before the Twelve Steps. He said he still felt they held good and could be extremely helpful when he wanted to do the right thing and the

answer was not obvious. "Almost always, if I measure my decision carefully by the yardsticks of absolute honesty, absolute unselfishness, absolute purity, and absolute love, and it checks up pretty well with those four, then my answer can't be very far out of the way," he said. The absolutes are still published and widely quoted at A.A. meetings in the Akron-Cleveland area.)[27]

Dr. Bob went to great length in his last major talk to A.A. at Detroit, Michigan, in December, 1948, to elaborate on the importance of the Four Absolutes and how he applied them.[28] In a letter he wrote to Howard C., Bill Wilson claimed he had included the Four Absolutes in Steps Six and Seven, and in the use of the word God.[29] But the language of A.A.'s Big Book shifted from "absolute" to less stringent "standards." The self-examination of the Big Book's "moral inventory" required looking for "resentments" and "grudges;" "selfishness" and "self-seeking;" "dishonesty;" "fears;" and the harms to others that accompanied them.[30] These, said the Big Book, were the common manifestations of ego-centricity, self-centeredness, and self-will run riot that blocked the alcoholic from God and left that person spiritually sick.[31] These were the subjects which were—in A.A.'s Fourth

---

[27] *DR. BOB and the Good Oldtimers* (New York: Alcoholics Anonymous World Services, Inc., 1980), pp. 54, 163. See also *Alcoholics Anonymous Comes of Age*, pp. 68, 75, 161; *Pass It On*, p. 127, 171-73; *The Language of the Heart* (New York: The A.A. Grapevine, Inc., 1988), pp. 196-200; Richmond Walker, *For Drunks Only* (MN: Hazelden, n.d.), Preface, p. 3; p. 6; Mel B., *New Wine: The Spiritual Roots of the Twelve Step Miracle* (MN: Hazelden, 1991), pp. 21, 41, 64, 76, 95, 98, 138, 139.

[28] *The Co-Founders of Alcoholics Anonymous: Biographical sketches. Their last major talks* (New York: Alcoholics Anonymous World Services, 1972, 1975), pp. 12-14.

[29] See Ernest Kurtz, *Not-God: A History of Alcoholics Anonymous*, exp. ed. (MN: Hazelden, 1991), pp. 242-43, 390 n. 22.

[30] Big Book: (1) Resentments and grudges, pp. 13, 64-67, 84, 86; (2) Selfishness and self-seeking, pp. 14, 61, 62, 67, 69, 84, 86; (3) Dishonesty, pp. 13, 28, 58, 65, 69, 70, 73, 84, 86; (4) Fear, pp. 62, 67, 68, 78, 84, 86; and (5) Harms to others, pp. 13, 67, 69, 70, 76, 77-84, 86.

[31] Big Book, pp. 64, 71, 72. See as to the Oxford Group definition of sin—"those sins which block us from God and from other people": Dick B., *The Oxford Group*, pp. 166-70.

Step, Tenth Step, and Eleventh Step inventories—to be listed on paper or in a daily review so they could be eliminated.[32]

Anne Smith was very practical in her treatment of the four absolute "yardsticks." And, long before the Twelve Steps were written, she wrote and taught about the manifestations of self that blocked people from God. The following were some of her comments:

> Emotion—anger, irritability, envy, jealousy, hurt feelings, self pity, sentimentality, which is enjoyment without responsibility, wasting emotions (pp. 17, 45).[33]
>
> Resentments to be faced and set right (p. 18).
>
> What makes us ineffective . . . resentments (p. 31).
>
> Fears—of inefficiency, incompetence, failing powers of application and success, about our body and its functions. Our minds, the way they work and the way they refuse to work; of infection, of serious illness, of a helpless and hopeless old age; of the loss of your husband's love, interpreting and misinterpreting his every movement, dreading every slight variation from the habitual routine of domestic life as a possible bringer of ill; afraid of what your children may do or be, or say, surrounding your whole family with an attitude of discomfort and nagging distrust of facing death; and of your secret self, of discouragement; and public speaking (pp. 17, 45).
>
> Our pride and fear . . . (p. 32).
>
> Fear and worry are atheism. And we have not left that behind when we take up this way of life. To be willing to be a fool for

---

[32] Big Book, pp. 64, 68-70, 84, 86.

[33] Compare the following in the Big Book: (1) We are then in much less danger of excitement, fear, anger, worry, self-pity, or foolish decisions, p. 88; (2) The greatest enemies of us alcoholics are resentments, jealousy, envy, frustration, and fear, p. 145.

Christ's sake is something different from being foolish.[34] Fear of poverty, illness, death, fear of people, fear of opinions (p. 37).

List of my sharing. Not costly—fear—worry—small conviction. Fear of what people would think of me. Hadn't faced myself honestly (p. 32).

How much place do fear and apprehension hold in my life (p. 50)?

I must let Christ run my life—always self before. Release from fear, timidity, inferiority. . . . Just a glimpse of a self-centered life. Fears as a child. Of trouble. Of what others thought. Of people (p. 53).

Telling a lie (pp. 18, 44).

Share dishonesty (p. 29).

Confession, Sharing with Another and Step Five

A.A.'s Fifth Step has a very clear origin in the Bible. That origin is James 5:16, which reads:

> Confess *your* faults one to another, and pray one for another, that ye may be healed. The effectual fervent prayer of a righteous man availeth much.[35]

---

[34] See 1 Corinthians 4:10: "We *are* fools for Christ's sake, but ye *are* wise in Christ; we *are* weak, but ye *are* strong; ye *are* honorable, but we *are* despised." See Shoemaker, *Children of the Second Birth*, pp. 65-80. Shoemaker devoted an entire chapter to "A Fool for Christ;" and this was one of the books Anne Smith highly recommended.

[35] See Dick B., *The Akron Genesis of Alcoholics Anonymous* (Kihei, HI: Paradise Research Publications, 1998), pp. 192-97, for a discussion of the impact of James 5:13-16 on the procedures early Akron AAs followed for prayer, healing, confession, and surrender.

The Fifth Step also suggests the confidential sharing of wrongs, shortcomings, and faults with another human being and with God. Anne Smith laid out these ideas in her Journal, saying:

> Confess your faults one to another. Sharing is having your life at God's disposal (p. 55).
>
> Sharing in Team Work. 1. Sharing the only basis of Scriptural team work. 3. Sharing builds a fellowship. 4. Sharing builds a team. 8. Honest sharing issues in action. 10. The only reason we don't share is because we cannot see the victory (p. 35).
>
> Positive reasons why we should share. 1. As we live a spiritual life, sharing becomes natural. 2. There is no adequate presentation of Christ without sharing our own sins. 3. We share because common honesty demands it. 4. Maximum usefulness demands it. Begin with known, and go on with the unknown. 5. It's the answer to loneliness. As we take down walls, we begin to give ourselves to others. 6. Because it's the basis of spiritual teamwork. The only answer to jealousy is to own up to it. Keep free of mental reservation and you begin to trust each other and become a spiritual power house for the community (p. 33).
>
> Kinds of Sharing. 1. Sharing for cure. 2. Sharing for release (confession). 3. Sharing for action. 4. Sharing for witness. 5. Sharing to build up fellowship in a team. 6. As restitution and a basis for honest living (p. 33).
>
> Principles of Sharing. 1. All sharing must be under guidance. 2. You do not tell everybody everything every time but you are ready to tell anybody anything at any time under guidance. 3. There is nothing in our lives that we are not willing to share. It is the quality of willingness. 4. Never betray a confidence. 5. Never share anybody else's sin. 6. Never involve another against his wishes. 7. No detailed confessions in public. 8. The extent of sharing in public should be co-extensive with the wrong done. If you have wronged a community, you must share in a community. 9. It is not enough to share the truth, but share truth in love. Ephesians 4:5. 10. Share specifically, uncomfortably so. 11.

Sharing in love without truth, sentimentality. Sharing truth without love, brutality. 12. Pray before you share, quietly. 13. We can make sharing with God alone a loophole, it may be too general. It is more definite with a person. 14. Sharing is a matter of being free from our own problems in order to be used by God. 15. Share your life completely with one person at a time, so that there is nothing that you have not shared with someone at some time (pp. 33-34).

Dangers of sharing: 1. Is it uncomfortable? 2. Is it dangerous to me, or my reputation, or to Christ? 3. The world is full of witness as to the dangers of not sharing, i.e., psychiatrists, ill health, nervous breakdowns, hospitals, bad theology, unbelief, spiritual impotency, divorce, asylums, broken homes, and lonely lives. The only danger really is when people live a half truth and begin to compromise (p. 34).

Sharing in relationship to the Gospel: 1. Matthew 3:6 Sins Confessed.[36] 2. Mark 1:5 Sins Confessed.[37] 3. Matthew 4:1-11 Christ shares his temptations.[38] 4. James 5:16 Share "My Life". Not confess ye one another's sins.[39] 5. Acts 26 Paul's defence

---

[36] Matthew 3:6 [Speaking of John the Baptist] "And were baptized of him in Jordan, confessing their sins."

[37] Mark 1:5 [Speaking of John the Baptist] "And there went out unto him all the land of Judaea, and they of Jerusalem, and were all baptized of him in the river of Jordan, confessing their sins."

[38] The account in Matthew 4:1-11 is of Jesus's being led up of the Spirit into the wilderness to be tempted of the devil. The devil came to Jesus, stating that if he (Jesus) were the Son of God, he could command stones to be made bread. But Jesus replied, quoting Scripture, and stated: "It is written, Man shall not live by bread alone, but by every word that proceedeth out of the mouth of God." Then the devil challenged Jesus to cast himself down from the pinnacle of the temple since it was written that God would give Jesus his angels to protect him. Again, Jesus quoted Scripture, stating, "It is written again, Thou shalt not tempt the Lord thy God." Finally, the devil offered Jesus all the kingdoms of the world and the glory of them if Jesus would fall down and worship him. Again Jesus quoted Scripture, telling the devil to "get thee hence," again stating, "for it is written, Thou shalt worship the Lord thy God, and him only shalt thou serve."

[39] James 5:16: "Confess *your* faults one to another, and pray for one another, that ye may be healed."

before Agrippa.[40] 6. 2nd. Cor 5:21 The inevitable sequence. Are we willing to become sinners in the eyes of our friends that they become righteous, putting the atonement into practice in life. "Greater love hath no man than this, that a man lay down his life for his friends," so that your friends may see how to live.[41]

Sharing . . . 2. All sharing must be redemptive. 3. Being honest to God, self and other people . . . 9. We share to prove that no one's problem is unique . . . 11. It is being honest even after it hurts. 12. It is giving your real self to another person. 13. How unnatural it is not to live a sharing life. 14. I start by rebelling against sharing, so talk it over with one other person. 15. Sins appear different under four eyes. 16. Sharing burns out the pride of self.

James—Confess your faults one to another 5:16 & pray one for another that ye may be healed (p. 32).

I must share to be honest with God, myself & others (p. 32).

---

[40] Acts 26 tells of Paul's answers to King Agrippa concerning charges against him. Paul said he would answer "all the things whereof I am accused of the Jews." He told of his youth, his life as a Pharisee, and of his standing, judged "for the hope of the promise made of God unto our fathers." He asked Agrippa "Why should it be thought a thing incredible with you, that God should raise the dead?" Paul said he had shut many saints up in prison, and gave voice against them so they would be put to death. He said he had persecuted them. Then he told of his conversion on the road to Damascus. He said Jesus had appeared to make him (Paul) a minister and a witness and sending him to the Gentiles to open their eyes, turn them from darkness to light, and from the power of Satan to God so they could receive forgiveness of their sins. He said he had told all they should repent and turn to God and that he was saying nothing that Moses and the prophets had not said concerning things to come. He then said his message was "That Christ should suffer, *and* that he should be first that should rise from the dead, and should shew light unto the people, and to the Gentiles." Paul asked Agrippa if he believed the prophets. Agrippa replied to Paul, "Almost thou persuadest me to be a Christian." Agrippa then declared Paul had done nothing worthy of death or of bonds.

[41] 2 Corinthians 5:21: "For he [God] hath made him [Christ] *to be* sin for us, who knew no sin; that we might be made the righteousness of God in him." Anne's quote about "Greater love hath no man" is from John 15:13: "Greater love hath no man than this, that a man lay down his life for his friends."

> Each confession a fresh humiliation breaks down another barrier. You can get to the place where you have nothing left to defend—that is release. You can go naked to God (p. 18).
>
> Inadequate sharing. We have not fully shared with some one else. Egoism or pride is one of the greatest of our enemies. Sharing with another under guidance roots it out (p. 16).
>
> Confession. Don't be shocked at any confession. It is hypocritical for you yourself have at least thought of doing something similar. A man may share many problems, but not his deepest one. You must share deeply with him, *under guidance* [italics in original]; You may be guided to share your deepest sin, and this will clear the way for him to share his. The time will come when he will begin to tell you things about himself that he doesn't tell to others (p. 4).

The Book of James was a favorite in early A.A.[42] James was considered so important that some early AAs suggested "The James Club" as a name for the A.A. Fellowship.[43] A.A. literature appears to confirm that James 5:16 was the foundation for its Fifth Step.[44] As shown above, Anne quoted this verse twice in her Journal in connection with admitting one's faults or sins. The Oxford Group quoted James 5:16 in the confession context.[45] And so did Sam Shoemaker.[46]

The concept of being honest with God, with another, and with yourself was a well established Oxford Group concept.[47] And what is noteworthy here is the remarkable similarity between the

---

[42] *DR. BOB*, pp. 71, 96; *Pass It On*, pp. 128, 138*n*, 147, 195.

[43] *Pass It On*, p. 147.

[44] *Pass It On*, p. 128.

[45] J. P. Thornton-Duesbury, *Sharing* (Pamphlet of The Oxford Group, published at Oxford University Press, n.d.), p. 5; Sherwood Sunderland Day, *The Principles of The Group* (Oxford: University Press, n.d.), p. 6; *What Is The Oxford Group?*, p. 29, 31.

[46] Shoemaker, *The Conversion of the Church*, p. 35.

[47] Shoemaker, *The Church Can Save the World*, pp. 110-12.

Big Book's Fifth Step language and that used by Anne Smith a number of years before the Big Book was written. We suggest the reader compare Anne's language above with the following in the Big Book:

> This [casting out the weak items in the moral inventory] requires action on our part, which, when completed, will mean that we have admitted to God, to ourselves, and to another human being, the exact nature of our defects. . . . This is perhaps difficult—especially discussing our defects with another person. We think we have done well enough in admitting these things to ourselves. There is doubt about that. In actual practice, we usually find a solitary self-appraisal insufficient. . . . Time after time newcomers have tried to keep to themselves certain facts about their lives.
>
> . . . Almost invariably they got drunk. . . . They took inventory all right, but hung on to some of the worst items in stock. They only *thought* they had lost their egoism and fear; they only *thought* they had humbled themselves. But they had not learned enough of humility, fearlessness and honesty, in the sense we find it necessary, until they told someone else *all* their life story. . . . Psychologists are inclined to agree with us. . . . We have seldom told them the whole truth nor have we followed their advice. Unwilling to be honest with these sympathetic men, we were honest with no one else. . . . We must be entirely honest with somebody if we expect to live long or happily in this world. Rightly and naturally, we think well before we choose the person or persons with whom to take this intimate and confidential step. . . . we search our acquaintance for a close-mouthed, understanding friend. . . . We pocket our pride and go to it, illuminating every twist of character, every dark cranny of the past (pp. 72-75, italics in original).

Conviction, Readiness to Be Changed and Step Six

The Oxford Group formulated the "Five C's."[48] They are mentioned in *DR. BOB and the Good Oldtimers* and other books about early A.A.[49] They—Confidence, Confession, Conviction, Conversion, and Continuance—were the heart of the Oxford Group's life-changing art. And A.A.'s own steps parallel these concepts.[50] A.A.'s Sixth Step concerned "repentance," or "willingness to be changed." Some, including this author, believe that the Oxford Group's "Conviction" idea was codified in A.A.'s Sixth Step.[51]

Anne had the following things to say about willingness to change and having God "remove" the defects of character uncovered in the moral inventory and confession (Fourth and Fifth Step) process:

> [Specifically discussing "The Five C's"] 3. Conviction. . . . Stay with him until he makes a decision and says it aloud (p. 4).

> In the early stages, win confidence. Think of meeting the other person's real needs. If you have a sense that something in him is not shared, it will block progress in meeting his real needs. It is like building a house and leaving huge boulders under it; you can't build a spiritual life for another without clearing the foundations. Many people go into tirades about sin in the national life, but

---

[48] See Dick B., *The Oxford Group*, pp. 175-79; Walter, *Soul Surgery*, pp. 21, 24, 28, 29; and Shoemaker, *Realizing Religion*, pp. 79-80.

[49] *DR. BOB*, p. 54; Walker, *For Drunks Only*, pp. 45-46; *The 7 Points of Alcoholics Anonymous*. Rev. ed. (Seattle: Glen Abbey, 1989), pp. 91-93.

[50] See Dick B., *The Oxford Group*, *supra*. Confidence had to do with Fifth Step sharing, and the Twelfth Step concept of working with others. Confession with the Fifth Step. Conviction with the Sixth Step. Conversion with the Third and Seventh Steps. And Continuance with A.A.'s so-called "maintenance" steps—Ten, Eleven, and Twelve—which are dedicated to maintaining and growing in the spiritual condition achieved by taking A.A.'s first nine steps.

[51] See Mel B., *New Wine*, pp. 34-35.

refuse to deal with it in their own life. Challenge them as to how much they really care about such situations (p. 5).

Lives depend on our openness to do God's will, a channel not a source. God more concerned than we. Need not fuss and stew if they don't yield if you are not right with God's will (p. 6).

Obedience is one of the key-words of the Christian life. Refusal to obey blocks the channel, and prevents further word from God (p. 16).

Barriers to a full surrender. 1. Is there anything I won't give up? 2. Is there any apology I won't make. . . . 13. Ideas about self—holding on to my own judgment of things, people, common sense and reason (p. 18).

Be willing to ask God where I am failing and to admit sin (p. 18).

Look out for denials, protests, self-justification, evasions, undue emotions (p. 25).

The next step is the Cross. Get them to the place where they appropriate it. Get them to face up to the thing that is their cross in life. Pray aloud with them. We cannot pray anyone else into the Kingdom. . . . It is not enough to surrender sin, but we must also claim the victory of the resurrection life. It is God that does it. Nothing you can do is of any use (pp. 25, 30).

Have you a Christ that can rid you of your sins and send you on your way rejoicing (p. 26)?

What is it that gives you the ability to make a right diagnosis? The fact that you have had a deep conviction yourself. . . . Do not be diverted from your main purpose of conquering sins. . . . If this is to happen, men have to have free minds, and to smash old modes of thought and points of view which have been built up on a rigid interpretation of the Bible. The Holy Spirit is ready to dictate a perfect plan (p. 19).

What makes us ineffective? 1. Trying to keep up appearances. 2. Pride in station of life. 3. Self pity—the most unnerving atmosphere in which one can live. 4. Memory of unshared sins: undone restitutions; possessions; unfulfilled guidance; self consciousness; unwillingness to surrender something; unwillingness to check plans with someone else; resentments; sentimental relationships; undue solicitude to find God's will (p. 31).

There are some definite barriers which we must recognize. There is also growth, and each day we see more and more things that need to be surrendered. A small sense of sin means a small sense of Christ. The closer you get to Christ, the more sensitive you become to sin. The whiter the cloth, the more easily it is stained (pp. 37, 56).

If there is anything in us which blocks God's work, it matters to God. Sin isn't merely an inconvenience to us, it is serious business. Keep your marginal areas free from sin in your life. Marginal areas of discipline must be so clear that you don't come within a mile of temptation. What are your marginal areas?—tongue, imagination. Be watchful always. John Wesley said, "Give me a hundred men who fear nothing but God and hate nothing but sin, and I will sweep the world" (p. 38).

It is because we have ignored sin in our presentation of the Gospel that the message of the Gospel has lost its sting and blasting power. Our first need is an emetic, not a narcotic. This emetic is facing the barrier, that is, our specific sins which are keeping us from Christ and from this complete and utter giving of ourselves to Christ. The real test of a surrendered life is that we are nice to live with. Surrender takes away the shams and gives us real life. Complete surrender brings us to the point where the most trivial of incidents will witness to the love of God. . . . You can't surrender sin if you won't admit it. . . . Be willing to admit a tendency to see ourselves as passions and instincts. The issue is to run away or surrender. Surrender to Christ or criticize the group. The welling up of criticism is the externalization of more sin (p. 42).

In its Sixth Step approach, the Big Book treats conviction in two installments. First, it suggests a *review* of Steps One through Five after the Fifth Step confession has been completed. It asks if anything has been omitted. It uses the metaphor of building a foundation—the same figure of speech Anne was using.[52] Then the book describes the Sixth Step itself in just one paragraph:

> We have emphasized willingness as being indispensable. Are we now ready to let God remove from us all the things which we have admitted are objectionable? Can He now take them all—every one? If we still cling to something we will not let go, we ask God to help us to be willing (p. 76).

As shown, Anne spoke mainly about facing up to the things that need to be changed, and then being willing to turn to God to be rid of these "sins."

Surrender of Sins, God's Removal and Step Seven

The life-change, the transformation, the conversion that took place when one "surrendered" and "gave his life to God" was much discussed and probably little understood in early A.A. But Oxford Group founder, Frank Buchman, made it simple for his followers. He spoke of "Sin, Jesus Christ, and the result, a miracle."[53] The miracle of the conversion seemingly could not, and did not need to be explained. Sam Shoemaker wrote in his first book:

> What you want is simply a vital religious experience. You need to find God. You need Jesus Christ.[54]

---

[52] For this figurative material, see Big Book, page 75.

[53] Frank Buchman often said, "Sin is the disease. Jesus Christ is the cure. The result is a miracle." See H. W. Bunny Austin, *Frank Buchman As I Knew Him* (London: Grosvenor Books, 1975), p. 10; Peter Howard, *Frank Buchman's Secret* (Garden City, NY: Doubleday & Co., 1961), p. 130; Walter, *Soul Surgery*, p 86.

[54] Shoemaker, *Realizing Religion*, p. 9.

Carl Jung, who was credited by AAs as suggesting their common spiritual solution, a conversion experience, wrote Bill Wilson, stating that the highest religious experience could be described as "the union with God." Jung quoted Psalm 42:1: "As the hart panteth after the water brooks, so panteth my soul after thee, O God."[55]

For Oxford Group people, who chose to speak in New Testament terms, surrender and conversion were rooted in John 3:3-8—being born again of the spirit.[56]

Anne Smith used a number of expressions pertaining to surrender and conversion; and they found their way into A.A. and its Big Book. She wrote:

> Conversion. This is the turning to God, the decision, the surrender (p. 4).
>
> A maximum experience of Jesus Christ leads to a radical change in personal life, bringing about a selfless relationship to people about one, which is a challenge to those we come in contact with (p. 29).
>
> God is willing to take my past spiritual experience and weld it in a new spiritual experience, God has spoken. The moment I hear and obey His voice and come to the place of complete surrender on every area of my life, is the moment of *rebirth*, reunion with Christ and a start on great revival campaign. *Rebirth*, reunion, revival involves decision, discipline and dare. . . . Surrender involves the explosive experience of a Holy Ghost conversion, the expulsive power of a new affection (p. 42, italics added).

---

[55] *Pass It On*, pp. 384-85.

[56] See Henry Drummond, *The Ideal Life* (New York: Hodder & Stoughton, 1897), p. 211; Frank Buchman, *Remaking the World* (London: Blandford Press, 1961), p. 23; Begbie, *Life Changers*, p. 104; Geoffrey Allen, *He That Cometh* (New York: Macmillan, 1932), pp. 19-43; Jones, *Inspired Children*, p. 136; Samuel M. Shoemaker, *National Awakening*, pp. 55, 57, 58; *Twice-Born Ministers*, pp. 56, 10; *By the Power of God* (New York: Harper & Brothers, 1954), pp. 28-33.

> [Speaking of sins such as possessiveness, temper, selfishness, dishonesty, and pride:] Christ can only *remove* them and replace with a new quality of life. Read Romans 12 (p. 36, italics added).[57]

> Those who have progressed farther than you feel the same need of that quiet time and from it find strength and power to do God's will (p. 47).

> Paul's advice. Stop trying to be good. Sounds dangerous. Really honest person knows he cannot reach goal of Goodness God desires. Face the truth. Do not pretend you can go on lifting yourself by your own boot straps. In all humility to God, "What would thou have me to do?" . . . I'm wrong Father. You know better than I, you have more wisdom, show me the way (p. 61).

In its "Seventh Step Prayer," the Big Book states:

> My Creator, I am now willing that you should have all of me, good and bad. I pray that you now *remove* from me every single defect of character which stands in the way of my usefulness to you and my fellows. Grant me strength, as I go out from here, to do your bidding. Amen (p. 76, italics added).

In its earlier discussion of surrender, the Big Book stated of God's power, will, and the rebirth:

> Being all powerful, He provided what we needed if we kept close to Him and performed His work well. . . . As we felt new power flow in, as we enjoyed peace of mind, as we discovered we could face life successfully, as we became conscious of His presence, we

---

[57] Oxford Group writer, Geoffrey Allen, said, in *He That Cometh*, that God can *remove* the things which fall short of the standard of fearless, spontaneous love, and which are symptoms of sin with which the devil may make us complacent (p. 147). Anne Smith recommended Allen's book in her Journal. Victor Kitchen, a popular Oxford Group writer in 1934 and a friend of Bill Wilson's, wrote, in *I Was a Pagan*, about God's *removing* selfish desire at the time of surrender. Kitchen said, "God simply lifted that desire entirely out of my life" (pp. 73-74).

> began to lose our fear of today, tomorrow or the hereafter. We were *reborn* (p. 63, italics added).[58]

Restitution, Amends and Steps Eight and Nine

As previously stated, Anne specified as one of the barriers to a full surrender, "Any restitution I won't make" (pp. 18, 43). She repeated this reference to setting things right and making restitution, listing "Resentments to be faced and set right" and "Restitution to be made" (pp. 18, 43). Then, in describing how to help people change, she wrote: "Help them make a list of things" (pp. 25, 29). Returning to the subject of amends, she wrote: "Restitution. In the matter of restitution, international retraction should be made by a positive, public statement equal in scope to the amount of damage done" (pp. 26, 51). On the topic of "willingness," she wrote:

> God can make me willing in the day of His power. Joy comes in being committed right to the very end. Attempt great things of God, and see the daily victories of the living God. This involves and enterprises discipleship under the guidance of the Holy Spirit, running up our colors, and helping others to run up theirs (p. 42).

As we point out, in our Chapter Four discussion of Oxford Group principles, Anne did not devote nearly as much space in her Journal to the restitution topic as she did to many other concepts which influenced A.A.

The Big Book said, as to amends and restitution (Steps Eight and Nine):

---

[58] See Dick B., *The Akron Genesis*, pp. 327-28, for a discussion of Bill Wilson's original language, in which Bill said, "For sure, I'd been born again." Compare the remarks of Bill's friend, Victor Kitchen, in *I Was a Pagan*. Kitchen spoke of the sensation of release and freedom for all who face and confess their sins and then said a surrender prayer similar to that in the Big Book, concluding, "We were reborn into life. . . ." (pp. 66-68).

> We have a list of all persons we have harmed and to whom we are willing to make amends. . . . We subjected ourselves to a drastic self-appraisal. Now we go out to our fellows and repair the damage done in the past. If we haven't the will to do this, we ask until it comes. . . . At the moment we are trying to put our lives in order. But this is not an end in itself. Our real purpose is to fit ourselves to be of maximum service to God and the people about us (pp. 76-77).
>
> Although these reparations take innumerable forms, there are some general principles which we find guiding. Reminding ourselves that we have decided to go to any lengths to find a spiritual experience, we ask that we be given strength and direction to do the right thing, no matter what the personal consequences may be. We may lose our position or reputation or face jail, but we are willing. We have to be (p. 79).

Continued Inventory, Daily Surrender and Step Ten

A.A.'s Tenth Step speaks to maintenance of the spiritual condition achieved through taking the previous nine Steps. It also challenges alcoholics "to grow in understanding and effectiveness." It says, "This is not an overnight matter. It should continue for our lifetime."[59]

For the Oxford Group and Sam Shoemaker, this involved the concept of "continuance" or "conservation"—the so-called fifth of the "Five C's."[60] In the Oxford Group/Shoemaker circles, in which early AAs were traveling, there were five aspects of "continuance": (1) Prayer; (2) Bible study; (3) Guidance; (4)

---

[59] See Big Book, pp. 84-85.

[60] See Begbie, *Life Changers*, p. 169 [calling the process "Continuance"]; Walter, *Soul Surgery*, pp. 89-100 [calling it "Conservation"]; and Shoemaker, *Realizing Religion*, pp. 79-80 [calling it "Conservation"].

Group worship; and (5) Witness.[61] They were part of the continuing process of "Daily surrender."[62]

Oxford Group writers had these things to say:

> Our lives will be one continuous surrender: surrender to God of every difficulty that confronts us, each temptation, each spiritual struggle, laying before Him either to take away or to show to us in their proper spiritual proportions.[63]

> When I came to make a daily surrender I learned what a different experience this is from a general surrender. Daily checking on the four absolutes revealed to me things I had never questioned in myself. . . . I came to a daily willingness to do anything for God. I made amends where He gave me light.[64]

> There is need for rededication day by day, hour by hour, by which progressively, in every Quiet Time, the contaminations of sin and self-will are further sloughed off (for they do have a way of collecting) and we are kept in fresh touch with the living Spirit of God. A further surrender is needed when and whenever there is found to be something in us which offends Christ, or walls us from another. We shall need, in this sense, to keep surrendering as long as we live.[65]

Anne was right on target with these ideas for maintaining the spiritual glow and growing in the application of spiritual principles. She wrote:

> Continuance. Stay with the newly surrendered person until he grows up and becomes a life-changer. Laugh him out of his growing pains.

---

[61] Dick B., *The Oxford Group*, pp. 293-97.

[62] Dick B., *The Oxford Group*, pp. 224-27.

[63] *What Is The Oxford Group?*, p. 46.

[64] Clarence Benson, *The Eight Points of The Oxford Group* (London: Oxford University Press, 1936), p. 149.

[65] Shoemaker, *The Conversion of the Church*, p. 79.

When he becomes a life-changer, we need not fear for him, because other people's needs will drive him back to God (p. 4).

Be willing to live a day at a time, an hour at a time (p. 9).[66]

3. What are the symptoms of let down or compromise in myself? . . . 5. Are quiet times increasingly real?. . . 7. Is there some relationship I am content to leave where it is? 8. Am I giving the right nurture to those changed? . . . 13. How much better do I know my Bible this year than last? . . . 14. Is my reading guided? (p. 10).

Be willing to ask God where I am failing and to admit sin. 1. Am I nicer to live with? 2. Better to work with? 3. More efficient with my job? (p. 18).

Paderewski [the famous concert pianist]: If I go one day without practicing the piano, I notice it in my playing; if I go two days my friends notice it; if I go three days the audience notices it (p. 31). Am I so living with God that Christ is being breathed around? You cannot sublimate an instinct that you don't recognize. You can't surrender sin if you don't admit it. A personal relationship with Jesus Christ depends on doing difficult things (p.42).

Willingness to maintain an antiseptic attitude with regard to personal situations while in the process of redemption. To be willing to face up that I alone am responsible for my attitude. Claim from God humility, patience, courage, faith, and love. These are gifts. We cannot qualify for them (p. 43).

Let your waking thought be surrender, a 100% daily surrender (p. 43).

After surrender [italics in original]: The difference is that when you discover sin and problems in your life, you know the answer,

---

[66] See our subsequent Eleventh Step discussion of *guidance* and Bill's uses of the "one day at a time" slogan.

> and you have the cure. There must be a focus of the issue when the mind is made up: then follows development. As we grow closer to Christ we keep seeing more sin, but we know the cure (p. 44).
>
> "Continue in the faith . . . and be not moved away from the hope of the Gospel." Colossians 1:23.[67]
>
> One of the weaknesses of what may be termed the "Old Evangelism" of the mass type was the lack of continuance. It seemed to be taken for granted that a surrendered person would naturally be able to continue what he had begun and would henceforth know of himself what the steps of strengthening should be. The truth is that many many people reached by the mass method did discover and take these steps, but it is safe to say that the majority fell by the wayside. The Oxford Group Movement believes strongly in Continuance. It further believes that every person (surrendered) needs careful nurture and help in life changing.

Anne devoted three pages to suggested steps for continuance (pp. 46-49). Here are the titles for the subjects Anne covered as to continuance; and we treat them in more detail in our Chapter Four:

1. Face the past for what it really was.
2. Burn all bridges behind you.
3. Witness to some friend who has come to you.
4. Practice daily surrender.
5. Daily Quiet Time.
6. Be alert for symptoms of let-down.
7. Blocks to Guidance.
8. Let all your reading be guided.
9. Let friends and relationships with others be guided.
10. Unite with a fellowship of kindred souls.
11. Don't try, but trust.

---

[67] Colossians 1:23: "If ye continue in the faith grounded and settled, and *be* not moved away from the hope of the gospel, which ye have heard, *and* which was preached to every creature which is under heaven; whereof I Paul am made a minister."

12. This quality of life is an adventure not an arrival.
13. Worth remembering.

The Big Book summarizes the Tenth Step process as follows: "Continued to take personal inventory and when we were wrong promptly admitted it" (p. 59). Its instructions for taking the step are more detailed:

> Continue to watch for selfishness, dishonesty, resentment, and fear. When these crop up, we ask God at once to remove them. We discuss them with someone immediately and make amends quickly if we have harmed anyone. Then we resolutely turn our thoughts to someone we can help. Love and tolerance of others is our code (p. 84).
>
> It is easy to let up on the spiritual program of action and rest on our laurels. We are headed for trouble if we do, for alcohol is a subtle foe. We are not cured of alcoholism. What we really have is a daily reprieve contingent on the maintenance of our spiritual condition. Every day is a day when we must carry the vision of God's will into all of our activities. "How can I best serve Thee—Thy will (not mine) be done." These are thoughts which must go with us constantly. We can exercise our will power along this line all we wish. It is the proper use of the will (p. 85).

Quiet Time, Prayer, Bible Study, Listening, God's Will, Guidance and Step Eleven

Prayer, Bible study, spiritual reading, listening for guidance, and the Quiet Time were supremely important in early A.A. Anne Smith was in the thick of sharing and teaching about them. But before we cover her notes, we think it important to record what others said of these subjects as they were practiced with success in early Akron A.A.:

> [Anne Smith's daughter, Sue:] After the Oxford Group, Mom didn't sit in the corner of the kitchen smoking so much. She

moved the ashtray to the telephone in the dining room. She spent a lot of time talking to her friends. She had that outlet. Later on, she did the same thing with the A.A. women. She did pass on the help that she received to the other women. And I [Sue Smith Windows] think that was the start of Al-Anon. I've still got Mom's notebook from the Oxford Group meetings. . . . If you read it, you'd see why Bill W. called her "the Mother of A.A.," and what I mean about my mom being the founder of Al-Anon. It's all there—share with people, don't preach, don't argue, don't talk up or down to people, share in terms of your own experience, be willing to live a day at a time, an hour at a time, surrender, pray for guidance, and have a daily meditation time.[68]

[Anne's daughter, Sue:] There was no program. Dad and Mom and Bill [Dr. Bob, Anne, and Bill Wilson] were working out the program. At that time I was getting involved with quiet times they had in the morning. The guys would come, and mom would have her quiet time with them. There was a cookie salesman and he'd bring the stale cookies over, and we'd take up a collection for three pounds of coffee for 29 cents. Then they'd have their quiet time, which is a holdover from the Oxford Group, where they read the Bible, prayed and listened, and got guidance. Then they'd have coffee and cookies. This was early in the morning, when the sky was just starting to get light. Sometimes they'd get us out of bed to do this.[69]

[Bill Wilson] Each morning, there was a devotion, he [Bill Wilson] recalled. After a long silence, in which they awaited inspiration and guidance, Anne would read from the Bible. "James was our favorite," he said. "Reading from her chair in the corner, she would softly conclude, 'Faith without works is dead.'"[70]

---

[68] Bob Smith and Sue Smith Windows, *Children of the Healer: The Story of Dr. Bob's Kids* (IL: Parkside Publishing, 1991), pp. 28-29.

[69] Smith and Windows, *Children of the Healer*, pp. 43-44. For details as to how meetings were conducted by Dr. Bob, by Bill D. (A.A. #3), and by Paul S., and opened with Bible study, see Dick B., *The Akron Genesis*, pp. 181-215.

[70] *DR. BOB*, p. 71.

Sue [Anne's daughter] also remembered the quiet time in the mornings—how they sat around reading from the Bible. Later, they also used The Upper Room, a Methodist publication that provided a daily inspirational message, interdenominational in its approach. "Then somebody said a prayer," she recalled. "After that, we were supposed to say one ourselves. Then we'd be quiet. Finally, everybody would share what they got, or didn't get. This lasted for at least a half-hour and sometimes went as long as an hour."[71]

[Anne's son, Robert R. Smith] was aware of the early-morning prayers and quiet time, but he didn't attend.[72]

[Henrietta D., wife of Bill D., A.A. #3,] remembered, "She [Anne Smith] would call me every single morning and ask me if I had had my quiet time. You were supposed to go by yourself with a pad and pencil and put down anything that came into your mind. Later in the day, it might come to you why. Probably for a year, she called me every single morning: 'Did you have your quiet time? Did you get anything special out it?' She was wonderful."[73]

[Paul S., an early Akron AA:] We had much prayer together in those days and began quietly to read Scripture and discuss a practical approach to its application in our lives.[74]

The A.A. members of that time [from 1935 to 1938] did not consider meetings necessary to maintain sobriety. They were simply "desirable." Morning devotion and "quiet time," however, were musts.[75]

---

[71] *DR. BOB*, pp. 72-73.

[72] *DR. BOB*, p. 72.

[73] *DR. BOB*, p. 86.

[74] *DR. BOB*, p. 110.

[75] *DR. BOB*, p. 136.

Morning quiet time continued to be an important part of the recovery program in 1938-1939, as did the spiritual reading from which the early members derived a good deal of their inspiration.[76]

Early AAs used to call their visits to the Smith's home, visits to get their "spiritual pablum."[77]

[As we wrote before, John R. of Akron remembered:] Before one of these meetings [in Dr. Bob's home], Anne used to pull out a little book [the "notebook" of which Sue Windows spoke, which we call Anne's "Journal"] and quote from it. We would discuss it. Then we would see what Anne would suggest from it for our discussion.[78]

And here are some of the specifics Anne wrote in her Journal and shared with others in the morning meetings, in the "spiritual pablum" visits, or on the phone:

1. *Prayer.*

Why not answered. Until we are ready to fulfil the conditions, the deepest wishes of our heart cannot be realized. . . . Intercessory prayer—pray that Spirit may tell you what to pray for. . . . A way to find God's will not to change it. Right orientation of soul toward God. Conceive God as Father and it is not unnatural to lay before Him our hopes and needs—interest—fears (p. 58).

Petitionary prayers. Expressions of sound instinct as long as we do not use to set right something for a grudging God. Means expression of our wants which we deeply feel and which it would be hypocrisy to pretend we didn't. These we submit not because we distrust His goodness or desire to bend His Will but because

---

[76] *DR. BOB*, p. 150.

[77] Dick B., *The Akron Genesis*, p. 110.

[78] Dick B., *The Akron Genesis*, p. 110.

He is our Friend. Similarly it would be unnatural not to submit to God the needs of others and our hopes and fears for them. If then we didn't find ourselves desiring to pray for them as we pray for ourselves we are not traveling in right direction (p. 58).

Intercessory prayer. If successful, weighty testimony. (p. 59).

Prayer for others to hold them before God, [?] to Him to give the thing they need but in spiritual concentration putting our personality, known or unknown, explained or unexplained, at His service. God's prayer—a trust in God—fellow man and myself. Correct me—direct—praise—adoration and thanksgiving. Romans II. God can guide thru other people (p. 59).

Difference [?] would make in attitude of prayer. Quiet approach of a child ready to receive. Not about our needs but taking matters to God and having communion with Him (Your Heavenly Father knows ye have needs of all these things).[79] More ready to hear than we to pray. Would to be shown spirit of prayer—gladness and faith (p. 6).

2. *Guidance*.

Guidance. Guidance is the principle of the Bible, its very structure. "God spoke" to Moses, to the prophets, to the Apostles. Paul was constantly guided by the Holy Spirit. Jesus was in constant touch with the Father. The Acts of the Apostles is called the Book of the Holy Spirit. The Bible is *guidance written down*. Modern theologians rule these things out of the Bible, because they don't realize that they still happen (Psalms 73 and 139). These things are in the background of the human race. The Constitution was written under Guidance. Hymn writers throughout the ages have realized guidance. The Holy Spirit is the

[79] From Matthew 6:33 in the Sermon on the Mount, "for your Father knoweth what things ye have need of, before ye ask him."

teacher. "He will guide you into all truth" (p. 8, italics in original).[80]

What are the conditions of receiving God's guidance? We must be in such relationship with God that He *can* guide us; He will not force Himself on us. The Sons of God are those who are guided by the Spirit of God. If we are wholly surrendered, we can absolutely count on guidance. Constant renewal of consecration is necessary. *Surrender is not an attitude attained; it is an attitude maintained*. The major condition is being absolutely willing and looking for God's direction in *all* things. We cannot receive guidance if we hold back an area, an habit, a plan. We must be alert to His direction in *Everything*; little things, as well as big ones such as career and marriage (p. 8, italics in original).

How does guidance come? Granted we are living so we can receive guidance, it comes to us in all the ways of human understanding. It could come in no other way. If God spoke in any other way we wouldn't understand it at all. Don't expect guidance in abnormal ways. Guidance is normal. Specifically, guidance comes through intelligent knowledge of the Bible, through *conscience* [italics in original], through *circumstance* [italics in original]. But some of us must surrender our conscience, because we are over conscientious. We always feel we must do the difficult or uncomfortable thing. God speaks through circumstance, but He may guide us to overcome circumstance. Guidance comes through reason and through common sense. Guidance is not a substitute for what you should do yourself. *guidance is thinking plus God* [italics in original]. God will guide us in many ways; through church; through Fellowship. The clearest guidance comes through a group, although we are not always willing to have another help us decide.[81] Guidance comes through direct intuitive thought.[82] Just

---

[80] From John 16:13, "Howbeit when he, the Spirit of truth, is come, he will guide you into all truth . . ."

[81] See A.A.'s Tradition Two, which reads: "For our group purpose there is but one ultimate authority—a loving God as He may express Himself in our group conscience. Our leaders are but trusted servants; they do not govern." Big Book, p. 564.

as we learn sometimes to know what a close friend is thinking, so we can really learn to think Christ's thoughts. Normal thoughts. The important thing is that they come with a sense of urgency enough for action. Guidance is not all black and white. But the more you give out to others, the more you will seek it (p. 8).

How can we proceed on guidance? A. Get the facts. B. *Expect* to be guided. When there are no barriers between you and God, you do expect guidance, and you act on the highest thought you have. God covers our mistakes in a marvelous way. We must not feel that there must be an overwhelming emotion. The basis of guidance is faith, not feeling, not analysis. Act on simple thoughts, and more will come.[83] So long as you keep on moving on the guidance you do get, you will get more. (Example of natives in a forest walking with lights on their feet; as long as they move forward, the lights shine on ahead; when they stop the light stops). Be willing to live a day at a time, an hour at a time.[84] C. Test your thoughts. It is possible to receive suggestions from your subconscious mind. Check your thoughts by the four standards of Christ; and by other guided persons. Each will have a part of the truth and thus make up the whole. Move forward as a phalanx. Act on the highest conviction that you have. It is well that we do not know what will happen a year ahead. Christ told his disciples He had many things to tell them—"But you cannot hear it now." Our course is guided by lighthouses. You may think you have been sent to a place for one reason, but when you are there you

---

[82] (...continued)

[82] See Big Book, p. 86, which states: "Here we ask God for inspiration, an intuitive thought or a decision."

[83] See Big Book, p. 87, which states, "What used to be the hunch or the occasional inspiration gradually becomes a working part of the mind. Being still inexperienced and having just made conscious contact with God, it is not probable that we are going to be inspired at all times. . . . Nevertheless, we find that our thinking will, as time passes, be more and more on the plain of inspiration. We come to rely upon it."

[84] For Bill's use of this expression, see *As Bill Sees It: The A.A. Way of Life . . . selected writings of A.A.'s co-founder* (New York: Alcoholics Anonymous World Services, 1967): (1) "Above all, take it one day at a time" (p. 11). (2) "One day at a time" (p. 317). (3) "The idea of 'twenty-four-hour living' applies primarily to the emotional life of the individual. Emotionally speaking, we must not live in yesterday, nor in tomorrow" (p. 284).

may find it is for another reason. D. Trust God fully for results. Walk by faith, not by sight. The Cross looks like a failure. Your guidance may look like a failure . . . (p. 9—italics in original).

We believe in television. Are you prepared to graduate in prayer? "I will lead you and guide you in all truth, and bring all thoughts to your remembrance" (John).[85] You will do three hours work in two hours if you live under guidance. Is your family worshipping on that basis? Have a wireless, out on which the whole family can tune in? "A spiritual aerial for every working home in England and the world." (Frank's [Frank Buchman's] message). [See p. 26 of Anne's Journal].

3. *Listening.*

Watch your thoughts. Your thoughts can come from three sources. 1. Subconscious. 2. The devil. 3. God. Your job to be a good signal man and know the difference between red and green lights. God's thoughts are—1. Not in conflict with the Bible. 2. Will stand the test of all four standards. 3. The test of circumstances. 4. The test of other guided people. 5. The test of action. If you have foolish thoughts, it is because you are foolish (unwise not ignorant). God is never capricious. Persevere till God's thought becomes your thought (p. 14, italics in original).

4. *Bible study and reading.*

Let all your reading be guided. [See our Chapter Three on the books Anne read and recommended]. . . . Of course the Bible ought to be the main Source Book of all. No day ought to pass without reading it. . . . *Let friendships and relationships with others be guided* . . . . When occasions arise which lead one into temptation, evasion is not the right way to meet them. Rather have a "Quiet Time" if possible before meeting them and go with a

---

[85] Compare what Jesus promised the "Comforter"—God's gift of holy spirit which would be given on the Day of Pentecost (Acts 2:1ff)—would do: see John 14:26 and John 16:13.

prayer in your heart. Lean on God and not on yourself (p. 16, italics in original).

5. *Quiet Time*.

Effective Quiet Time: 1. Objective, God and obedience. 2. Attentive prayer and being willing to act immediately. 3. Stillness and surrender of all known sins. *Results of an effective Quiet Time*: 1. Overflowing life. 2. Attitude made clear. 3. Strength for everything. No guidance in the world leaves you out of power and the presence of God (p. 44, italics in original).

Daily Quiet Time: This cannot be emphasized too much. Not a day should be missed. The early morning hours are best. It may be that more than one quiet time will be needed during the day. Whenever need arises one should stop and pray and listen. The method of holding quiet time varies some with each individual. All include prayer and Bible reading and study and patient listening to God. If you have difficulty in getting help in quiet time, go to some surrendered person and share the difficulty. Those who have progressed farther than you feel the same need of that quiet time and from it find strength and power to do God's will. How much more then a beginner needs it. In quiet we close the switch between us and God from which Power and Guidance come. If that switch is not closed by you, that Power and Guidance cannot come (p. 47, italics in original).

Be alert for symptoms of let-down. . . . One of the first of these symptoms is a sudden disgust with "the whole business" and feeling that it is the "bunk." It is your own soul that is in a funk. Other symptoms of let-down are: No guidance seems to come in Quiet Time, or what guidance does come is too vague; or the guidance received does not seem to work out rightly. Note the blocks to guidance below. Share with a more mature surrendered person. Never give up. A child does not learn to walk in a day. The feeling "What's the use" that comes when you failed or slipped in the face of a challenge or did not follow the guidance you received. You may be too confident in your own strength. Remember that you do not change your inner life. God changes it.

> He must be kept constantly in the center of life as He is seen in Christ. The answer to this feeling is prayer and new surrender. Lean on Christ, not on yourself. The feeling of revulsion after you have really shared in a meeting or with an individual your change. Sometimes people feel that they have "made a fool of themselves." This feeling of revulsion must be given up. Self is in the center of it and not Christ. This feeling is the grip of the old life seeking to hold you, or if you prefer, The Devil fighting to keep you for his own (p. 47, italics in original).
>
> What to do in these moments is rather simple. Get down on one's knees and give up completely to Christ and His will for you, remembering that anything that pulls you down is your enemy while God is your best friend in the world. Recall that the new life is infinitely better than the old. If release does not come anew, go to some surrendered person and share the "let down." Have a Quiet Time and prayer together, and you will find release again (p. 48).

We believe the Big Book's instructions for taking the Eleventh Step can be divided into four parts. The actual Eleventh Step language suggests that AAs, "sought through prayer and meditation to improve our conscious contact with God *as we understood Him*, praying only for knowledge of His will for us and the power to carry that out." Its four sets of instructions for taking this Step might be categorized in the following manner.

First, those things the AA is to do each evening as he or she constructively reviews the day (p. 86). In effect, AAs are to review how well they practiced the Tenth Step during their daily surrender process. The review questions are: (1) "Were we resentful, selfish, dishonest or afraid?" [a Step Four question]; (2) "Do we owe an apology?" [a Step Nine question]; (3) "Have we kept something to ourselves which should be discussed with another person at once?" [a Step Five question]; (4) "Were we kind and loving toward all? What could we have done better? Were we thinking of ourselves most of the time? Or were we thinking of what we could do for others, of what we could pack into the stream of life?" [Steps Four, Six, Seven and Twelve questions] . . . (5) "After making our review we ask God's forgiveness and inquire what corrective measures should be taken." While these hardly seem to qualify as "prayer and meditation," they are part of A.A.'s Eleventh Step instructions. And we have seen from Anne's Journal how frequently she posed tests for determining how well a person was conducting daily surrender and quiet time activities.

Second, the Eleventh Step places great focus on how one commences the day (pp. 86-87). Recall that Anne Smith spoke of living "one day at a time." The Big Book suggests, "On awakening, let us think about the twenty-four hours ahead. We consider our plans for the day." It then suggests three different approaches: (1) That we ask God to direct our thinking and keep the thought-life clear of wrong motives. [This certainly coincides with Anne's emphasis on, and discussion of guidance, quiet time, prayer, listening for leading thoughts, and checking.] (2) That we ask God for inspiration, an intuitive thought or a decision when facing "indecision." [The relevance of Anne's prayer and meditation comments seems clear to us.] (3) That we be shown all through the day what the next step is to be, that our needs be supplied in that regard, and that our actions be free from selfish ends. [Again, Anne's comments comprehend this subject matter.]

Third, the Eleventh Step process covers what the author has often described as the Big Book's "lost paragraph;" and, more optimistically, the "growth paragraph." We call this the *growth* paragraph because Bill Wilson frequently spoke of A.A. as a "spiritual kindergarten."[86] In the Big Book's "spiritual growth" paragraph, Bill wrote as follows:

> If circumstances warrant, we ask our wives or friends to join us in morning meditation. If we belong to a religious denomination which requires a definite morning devotion, we attend to that also. If not members of religious bodies, we sometimes select and

---

[86] See, for example, *As Bill Sees It*, p. 95.

> memorize a few set prayers which emphasize the principles we have been discussing. There are many helpful books also. Suggestions about these may be obtained from one's priest, minister, or rabbi. Be quick to see where religious people are right. Make use of what they offer (p. 87).

We believe many portions of our book demonstrate Anne's influence on the foregoing paragraph. Anne's whole family, and those—including Bill Wilson—who visited her home, were involved in a great deal of morning meditation. Anne and Dr. Bob maintained membership in a religious denomination for most of the period from 1935 to the end of their lives. Anne suggested specific prayers in her Journal. She recommended and used the Bible, many spiritual books, and daily Bible devotionals as part of the daily inspirational reading. And she suggested seeking help from others as to the materials which should be read.

Finally, the Big Book speaks of the action to be taken throughout the day when agitated or in doubt. Essentially, it recommends seeking the guidance of God and surrendering to him many times throughout the day, saying, "Thy will be done" (pp. 87-88). Anne's paralleled all aspects of these latter suggestions.

The Spiritual Awakening, Witness, Practice of Principles and Step Twelve

Professor William James, the Oxford Group, and Reverend Sam Shoemaker had many expressions for the "vital religious experience" or "conversion" which took place when a person surrendered his or her life to God, took the steps of confession, conviction, conversion, restitution, and continuance, and then experienced the fruits of the changed life. As we discuss in Chapter Four, the religious experience was variously described as: (1) An experience of God. (2) A vital experience of Jesus Christ. (3) A religious experience. (4) A spiritual experience. (5) A spiritual awakening. (6) A relationship with God. (7) A sense of the power and presence of God. (8) Finding God. (9) Being in touch with

God. (10) Contact with God. (11) Conversion. (12) Surrender. (13) Change. (14) Born again. (15) God Consciousness.[87]

Anne discussed most of these synonymous ideas; and she wrote much on Christian Witness and living by spiritual principles, particularly those of the Four Absolutes.

We believe A.A.'s Twelfth Step can and should be viewed as having three "parts." They are: (1) The spiritual awakening obtained as the result of taking the preceding eleven steps. (2) The obligation to witness to others by "passing on" the message of how one received deliverance through God. (3) The actual living of a changed life by "practicing the principles"—the principles learned from taking the twelve steps of recovery.

We will discuss Anne's writing concerning Twelfth Step ideas under the aforementioned three topics.

1. *The Spiritual Awakening.*

As we've shown, Anne adopted William James's definition of "conversion"—the one so often quoted by Reverend Sam Shoemaker. But the attributes of a spiritual awakening were covered by her in substantial detail:

> A general experience of God is the first essential, the beginning. We can't give away what we haven't got. We must have a genuine contact with God in our present experience. Not an experience of the past, but an experience of the present—actual, genuine. When we have that, witnessing to it is a natural, just as we want to share a beautiful sunset. We must be in such close touch with God that the whole sharing is guided. The person with a genuine experience of God and with no technique will make fewer mistakes than one with lots of technique, and no sense of God. . . . We must clearly see and understand our own experience (p. 2).
>
> Conversion. This is the turning to God, the decision, the surrender (p. 4).

---

[87] See Dick B., *The Oxford Group*, pp. 275-85.

Creation of spirit of man. Made that spirit part of himself. Own spirit in us. Made man incomplete in his soul, so that he never finds such peace and happiness apart from God as he finds in him. Prophets helped find God. His Son in the fullness of time when all else went awry. Herein is love, not that we loved God but that He loved us and sent His Son to be propitiation of our sins. 1 John 4:10. God tries to reach down to us, and we [?] to reach Him. Made us free to choose—represents our freedom. Projects us so much light as we can stand. Gives us as much as we can comprehend. Reveals all we can grasp. Let perfection down into world—lest it dazzle our sight and we go blind. Observance wrapped in the body of baby. Many of God's approaches are small, still, ourselves. Jesus human in all points belongs to natural order spiritual [?] God in His character. Humanity apparent—divinity evident in Him. Humanity approaches God through a perfect High Priest, in Him God visited man as through a perfect reminder (p. 6).

(Kagawa) Even the Christian church of today misunderstands Christ here. The purpose of our having mystical experience is not that we may achieve our own personal satisfaction, but that we may succor the poor, help those who are in trouble, and educate the masses (p. 20).

(Elinor Forde) [*sic*] A maximum experience of Jesus Christ leads to a radical change in personal life, bringing about a selfless relationship to people about one, which is a challenge to those we come in contact with (pp. 25, 29).

Crucifixion is open to the world so that anyone can see it was a public atonement. Sharing is a simple transparency. It is a sick world—the remedy rests on Christ himself, the healer of the world (p. 35).

The decision to give my life to Christ involves discipline to keep a quiet time as my first waking act . . . (p. 42).

We do not go into the quiet time to get guidance but to realize a Presence and the mighty love of God (p. 43).

> Claim victory, power, purpose, to become free children of God; victory in the department of the mind, no slavery, no effort (self), no judging of guidance by results (p. 44).
>
> *Don't try, but trust*. Any kind of goodness that you try to achieve with effort will be self-righteousness which has self in the center. That is why it is repellent. "Not having mine own righteousness" is Paul's phrase.[88] The only effort we need to put forth is that of daily surrender and daily contact with Christ. We find release not by our own efforts but by what Christ does for us and in us when we open every area of our lives to him (p. 49, italics in original).
>
> *The quality of life is an adventure not an arrival*. We surrender to God from more and more and from more to maximum. As E. Stanley Jones says, "Christianity is an *obtainment* not an attainment and the more we obtain, the more we see there is to obtain." Maturity comes from fuller self renunciation and surrender and often it takes new experience to bring us farther along the way. The goal is "Be ye therefore perfect, even as your Father in Heaven is Perfect" (p. 49, italics in original).[89]
>
> When Paul gave up trying to be good and surrendered his life fully to the Lord, then came peace, power and joy (p. 61).
>
> God's gift in Christ is gladness and humility. This goodness not my own will spring up in me in amazing strength and power. I will go through the world with a song in my heart because God so loved the world and me (p. 62).

Compare the following ideas in A.A.'s Big Book:

> There was a sense of victory, followed by such a peace and serenity as I had never known. There was utter confidence. I felt

---

[88] See Philippians 3:9, "And be found in him [Christ], not having mine own righteousness, which is of the law, but that which is through the faith of Christ, the righteousness which is of God by faith."

[89] Compare Matthew 5:48 in the Sermon on the Mount.

lifted up, as though the great clean wind of a mountain top blew through and through. God comes to most men gradually, but His impact on me was sudden and profound (Bill's Story, p. 14).

The great fact is just this, and nothing less: That we have had deep and effective spiritual experiences which have revolutionized our whole attitude toward life, toward our fellows and toward God's universe (p. 25).

[It] is true that our first printing gave many readers the impression that these personality changes, or religious experiences, must be in the nature of sudden and spectacular upheavals. Happily for everyone, this conclusion is erroneous. . . . Most of our experiences are what the psychologist William James calls the "educational variety" because they develop slowly over a period of time. . . . With few exceptions our members find they have tapped an unsuspected inner resource which they presently identify with their own conception of a Power greater than themselves. Most of us think this awareness of a Power greater than ourselves is the essence of a spiritual experience. Our more religious members call it "God-consciousness" (pp. 571-72).[90]

In the face of collapse and despair, in the face of the total failure of their human resources, they found that a new power, peace, happiness, and sense of direction flowed into them. . . . When many hundreds of people are able to say that the consciousness of the Presence of God is today the most important fact of their lives, they present a powerful reason why one should have faith (pp. 50-51).

In a few seconds he was overwhelmed by a conviction of the Presence of God. . . . He stood in the Presence of Infinite Power and Love. He had stepped from bridge to shore. For the first time, he lived in conscious companionship with his Creator (p.56).

[90] For the frequency with which this term was used in Oxford Group circles, see Dick B., *The Oxford Group*, p. 277.

> We will suddenly realize that God is doing for us what we could not do for ourselves (p. 84).

> Much has already been said about receiving strength, inspiration, and direction from Him who has all knowledge and power. If we have carefully followed directions, we have begun to sense the flow of His Spirit into us. To some extent we have become God-conscious (p. 85).

> As Him in your morning meditation what you can do each day for the man who is still sick. The answers will come, if your own house is in order. But obviously you cannot transmit something you haven't got. See to it that your relationship with Him is right, and great events will come to pass for you and countless others. This is the Great Fact for us (p. 164).

2. *Witness—giving it away to keep it.*

A large part of Anne's Journal was devoted to sharing with, and service to, others; life-changing; and "witnessing." She said:

> Giving Christianity away is the best way to keep it (p. 64).

> We can't give away what we haven't got (p. 2).

> When we have that [a general experience of God], witnessing to it is natural, just as we want to share a beautiful sunset. . . . Share with people—don't preach, don't argue. Don't talk up nor down to people. Talk to them, and share in terms of their own experiences, speak on their level (p. 2).

> People reveal themselves and their problems by: 1. *Silence*. A sudden silence indicates that you have touched some real problem. 2. *Talkativeness*. Sometimes they filibuster so that you know they would not talk so much unless there was something they didn't want to say. 3. *Nervousness*. That goes back to some unsurrendered, unshared thing in their lives. Nervousness generally comes from an inner conflict. Watch the hand. You will be able to see

that this person is hopelessly divided inside; a divided personality. 4. *Criticism* [italics in original]. In order not only to answer criticism, but to meet the needs of others, we must acquire the knowledge, first, that what the Groups teach is Biblical; second, of what psychology teaches. It is sometimes difficult to answer criticism, because it has to do not only with our own mistakes, but with things beyond our control. Dr. Grensted says this is due to the principles of "projection."[91] People project upon a group or upon another person, some problem they themselves have. (Examples: two ladies had their first glass of champagne, and it was too much for them. One said indignantly to the other, "You are intoxicated; you've got two noses.") People will project upon you the things they hate in themselves. It is important to understand this principle of projection. Much criticism is second-hand gossip. The way to meet it is to say, "Come and see" (p. 3, italics in original).[92]

Confidence. We need to make friends with people first. Get a person to talk about his interests. Reverence what other people reverence; don't stifle the truth they have, but lead on from that. (Example: the atheist who finally said he believed in helping people;—an excellent beginning point.) Make points of contact through reading people, with outright sinners, and with intellectual leaders like Nicodemus.[93] Learn to feel at home with all sorts of people. Learn to intrigue people with stories of individual lives that have been changed. Tell a business man how a business man has been changed, and how he finds it works in his business (p. 4).

How to interview. Jesus's talk with the Samaritan woman at the well (John 4). Jesus was exhausted, but the woman's need challenged him. We may suddenly be confronted with someone's

---

[91] Dr. L. W. Grensted was a distinguished Oxford Group adherent and theologian who wrote several titles popular in the Oxford Group. See Dick B., *The Oxford Group*, pp. 104-05; *New Light on Alcoholism*, p. 321. Grensted wrote the foreword to *What Is The Oxford Group?*

[92] See the account of witnessing among Jesus Christ's apostles in John 1:46.

[93] See John chapter three.

need when we are tired. "Give me to drink." The natural approach. Jesus guided the conversation naturally where He wanted it. After He had aroused her curiosity, she asks, "Where do you get this living water?" Don't be too serious with people; intrigue them, play with them if they want to play; learn how to talk about things they are interested in—fishes to fishermen, water to the woman drawing water. "Will become a spring of water"—a positive statement. We must be positive about what we know from our experience works. "How can I get it?"—the crux of the interview. "Go call your husband"—Jesus goes straight to her sin (p. 5, italics in original).

Winning others. In the early stages, win confidence. Think of meeting the other person's needs. If you have a sense that something in him is not shared, it will block progress in meeting his real needs (p. 5, italics in original).

For that which we have seen and heard declare we unto you that ye also may have fellowship with us—and truly our fellowship is with the Father and with His Son, Jesus Christ.[94] 1st fellowship came to me when others witnessed how Christ had changed their lives. That made me want first the joy and release they had. Then came 2nd Step—how rotten—resentful—picked flaws—hard for me to be honest about myself—the flaws I picked were ones I had in my own life. 3rd—fellowship with Christ means living His work—the human fellowship is as natural by [?] and its so very sweet and comes proportionately as I give. Read further in John III:2 [*sic*]—Beloved I wish above all things that thou mayest prosper and be in health, even as thy soul prospereth. . . . Imagine the President speaking over a nation-wide hookup saying: My fellow citizens, my best wish for you is that your material prosperity and your physical health may be just in proportion to your spiritual well-being (pp. 11-12).

What should come into a witness. Conciseness. Talking in pictures. Get to some apex—the one thing you want to get across.

---

[94] See 1 John 1:3.

Humour—A light touch should come in. Concrete instances rather than vague statements. Paint pictures of the new life more forcibly than the old. Relate your witness to one person in the crowd. Learn to chisel your witness to different people. Learn to hang it on any hook, and make it illustrate principle. *Ten suggestions for personal work*: 1. Get a point of contact. 2. Diagnose the person's real difficulty. 3. Make the moral test (4 standards). 4. Avoid argument. 5. Aim to conduct the interview yourself. 6. Adapt the truth to the hearer's need. 7. Bring the person face to face with Christ. 8. Show the way out of the special difficulty. 9. Bring the person finally to the point of decision and action. 10. Start the person on the new life with simple, concrete and definite suggestions, regarding Bible study, prayer, overcoming temptation and service to others (p. 14, italics in original).

(KAGAWA) Christ's basic principle, which he expressed in saying that we must love even the very least of them, did not arise from his teaching, neither did it come from his practice. It grew out of the fact that he had entered into the consciousness of God.[95] The consciousness of atonement, that is the conscious sharing of the atoning purposes of God.[96] Whoever would bear responsibility for others must have sympathies broad enough to include the failures, the human derelicts. He has not entered into the consciousness of God who looks at some mean fellow whom society counts worthless, and says, "Oh that fellow he's hopeless; he's just a good-for-nothing!" The nearer to God we come, the more conscious we grow of our responsibility towards those worthless folk who are regarded as the very dirt under one's feet. If we ask why it was that Christ always chose the worthless folk, it was because he possessed a one hundred per cent consciousness of God; he shared to perfection his own consciousness of the redemptive purpose of God (p. 19).

---

[95] Anne's notes use the word "conscienceness," but we believe this was an error which occurred in typing from her hand-written material. We believe, from the context of her writing, and from the sources upon which she relied, that she spoke of "consciousness."

[96] See previous footnote.

In one of his earliest pamphlets—one which Anne quoted in her spiritual journal—Sam Shoemaker spoke of "giving it away to keep it."[97] The following, from a much later Shoemaker book, exemplifies this concept of "passing it on." Shoemaker wrote:

> The best way to keep what you have is to give it away, and no substitute has ever been found for personal Christian witness.[98]

Compare the following thoughts from A.A.'s Big Book:

> He [Bill Wilson] suddenly realized that in order to save himself he must carry his message to another alcoholic (p. xvi).

> My friend [Bill Wilson's sponsor, Ebby Thacher] had emphasized . . . [that it was] imperative to work with others as he had worked with me. Faith without works was dead, he said. And how appallingly true for the alcoholic! For if an alcoholic failed to perfect and enlarge his spiritual life through work and self-sacrifice for others, he could not survive the certain trials and low spots ahead (p. 15).

> Practical experience shows that nothing will so much insure immunity from drinking as intensive work with other alcoholics. It works when other activities fail. This is our *twelfth suggestion*: Carry this message to other alcoholics! (p. 89).

> And be careful not to brand him as an alcoholic (p. 92).

> Keep his attention focussed mainly on your personal experience. . . . Tell him exactly what happened to you. Stress the spiritual feature freely (pp. 92-93).

---

[97] Samuel M. Shoemaker, *One Boy's Influence* (New York: Association Press, 1925), p. 15.

[98] Samuel M. Shoemaker, Jr., *They're on the Way* (New York: E. P. Dutton, 1951), p. 159. See also Dick B., *New Light on Alcoholism: The A.A. Legacy from Sam Shoemaker* (CA: Good Book Publishing, 1994), p. 274.

> It is important for him to realize that your attempt to pass this on to him plays a vital part in your own recovery. . . . Suggest how important it is that he place the welfare of other people ahead of his own (p. 94).
>
> You will be most successful with alcoholics if you do not exhibit any passion for crusade or reform. Never talk down to an alcoholic from any moral or spiritual hilltop; simply lay out the spiritual tools for his inspection. Show him how they worked with you. Offer him friendship and fellowship. Tell him if he wants to get well you will do anything to help (p. 95).
>
> Helping others is the foundation stone of your recovery (p. 97).
>
> The minute we put our work on a service plane, the alcoholic commences to rely upon our assistance rather than upon God. . . we simply do not stop drinking so long as we place dependence upon other people ahead of dependence on God. Burn the idea into the consciousness of every man that he can get well regardless of anyone. The only condition is that he trust God and clean house (p. 98).
>
> Remind the prospect that his recovery is not dependent upon people. It is dependent upon his relationship with God (p. 100).
>
> Give freely of what you find and join us (p. 164).

3. *Living the changed life practicing the spiritual principles.*

Many claim Anne Smith's "favorite" Bible verse was "Faith without works is dead."[99] The verse certainly wound up in A.A.'s Big Book (pp. 14, 76, 88). And Anne wrote much about *living* by spiritual principles.

The Big Book really does not define the "principles" or "works" in any orderly fashion. But we think the following are

[99] See Nell Wing, *Grateful to Have Been There* (IL: Parkside Publishing, 1992), pp. 70-71; *DR. BOB*, p. 71; *Pass It On*, p. 147.

among the principles to be practiced: (1) Reliance upon God (pp. 46, 50, 51-53, 68, 80, 98, 100, 120, 292); (2) Rigorous honesty (pp. 58, 64, 67, 69, 73, 84, 86); (3) Elimination of selfishness and self-centeredness (pp. 62, 63, 69, 84, 86); (4) Elimination of resentment, jealousy, and envy (pp. 64-67, 84, 86, 145); (5) Elimination of fear (pp. 67-68, 84, 86, 145); (6) Practicing patience, tolerance, kindliness, understanding, love, forgiveness, and helpfulness to others (pp. 20, 77, 83, 84, 97, 118, 153, 292).

The Oxford Group's "Four Absolutes"—honesty, purity, unselfishness, and love—are not mentioned as "absolutes" in the Big Book, but were "yardstick" principles by which early AAs measured their conduct.[100] And the concepts of honesty, unselfishness, and love are very much a part of A.A. thinking.

We have already covered many of Anne's remarks about spiritual principles, but the following are additional specifics:

> *Faith* [italics in original]. Go ahead on faith, not feelings. Emotion is the fruit and not the root of your faith. It may or it may not come. Jesus continually puts the emphasis on faith. . . . If you have given your life to God, trust Him and go ahead with that (p. 2).

> Proceed with imagination and real faith—expect things to happen. If you *expect* things to happen, they *do* happen. This is based on *faith in God*, not on our own strength. A negative attitude toward ourselves or others cuts off God's power; it is evidence of lack of faith in His power. If you go into a situation admitting defeat, of course you lose (p. 2—italics in original).

> We must keep before us the maximum perspective of our task as Christians. (John 15:13-17). . . . You must be willing to lay down alongside another's [life] perhaps for years (p. 2).[101]

---

[100] *DR. BOB*, p. 54.

[101] John 15:13-17: "Greater love hath no man than this, that a man lay down his life for his friends. Ye are my friends, if ye do whatsoever I command you. Henceforth I call (continued...)

You can count on people who stay with you in a movement like this, because they stay with you for God's sake, and not for popularity's sake (p. 3).

Stay with the newly surrendered person until he grows up and becomes a life-changer. Laugh him out of his growing pains. When he becomes a life-changer, we need not fear for him, because other people's needs will drive him back to God (p. 4).

How can we do the maximum job that God will have us do (p. 15)?[102]

Christ's basic principle, which he expressed in saying that we must love even the very least of them, did not arise from his teaching, neither did it come from his practice. It grew out of the fact that he had entered into the consciousness of God (p. 19).

(Elinor Forde) [*sic*] Foundation of this Philosophy. A maximum experience of Jesus Christ leads to a radical change in personal life, bringing about a selfless relationship to people about one, which is a challenge to those we come in contact with. . . . No one can do for me what Jesus Christ has done for me. . . . Fellowship of love must exceed fellowship of hate and be just as demanding. . . . No criticism. No slumping with tongue (pp. 25, 26).[103]

---

[101] (...continued)
you not servants; for the servant knoweth not what his lord doeth: but I have called you friends; for all things that I have heard of my Father I have made known unto you. Ye have not chosen me, but I have chosen you, and ordained you, that ye should go and bring forth fruit; and *that* your fruit should remain: that whatsoever ye shall ask of the Father in my name, he may give it you. These things I command you, that ye love one another."

[102] Compare Big Book, p. 77: "Our real purpose is to fit ourselves to be of maximum service to God and the people about us."

[103] Dr. Bob frequently spoke of guarding that erring member, the tongue. See *DR. BOB*, p. 338. Anne often spoke to the same effect in her Journal. Considering the (continued...)

Being honest to God, self and other people. . . . It is being honest even after it hurts. It is giving your real self to another person (p. 34).

Do we condemn, condone, or construct (p. 35)?

Little sins: 1. Possessiveness—holding on to what one has. A fear of not hating sin enough, self-justification, excusing oneself. 2. Moods and manners, giving way to feelings, temper, irritability, want of control. 3. Getting one's own back, evil for evil, self-opinionated. . . . 5. Forcing one's own opinion—unkind tongue, cutting answers, scandal, exaggeration, enlarging when speaking, looking down others. 6. Self-pity. Listen to others' troubles, your own disappear. . . . 9. Being selfish and scheming with friends. . . . 11. Branding certain races of people (Ephesians 1:2, 3). 12. Self-consciousness—conceit. . . . 15. Petty dishonesties. 16. Borrowing and not returning. 17. Pilfering. . . 18. Asserting rights. Show kindness. 19. Liking people who like you and not liking people who don't appeal to you. . . . 21. Pride of race, face, place and grace. 22. Christ can only remove them and replace with a new quality of life. Read Romans 12. . . . 24. Idolatry—worship other things but God, other people, ourselves, such practices as we have found to work. . . 27. Timidities—Being shy, fear. 28. Self-pity—wasting time over self when we ought to be taking full responsibility. . . . 30. Self-dependence–Indispensability, self-importance, letting sin come between us and the work God intends us to do (p. 36, italics in original).

Good People's Sins: . . . Impatience with people and circumstances. . . . Indiscipline of tongue (James 3). . . Fear and worry, are atheism. . . . Fear of poverty, illness, death, fear of people, fear of opinions. Intolerance: We must be free of intolerance toward classes, races, and points of view. If you feel you have to

---

[103] (...continued)
popularity of the Book of James with Dr. Bob, Anne, and the Akron AAs, we have little doubt that the emphasis came from James 3:1-18. Thus James 3:8 states: "But the tongue can no man tame; *it is* an unruly evil, full of deadly poison."

defend something, it is something in yourself. We don't have to defend a point of view. This way of living is not a point of view to be defended. It is a life to be shown. Christ needs not defense, but proclamation (p. 37).

Worry about money leads into all sorts of terrible mistakes, and into fear. . . . Live more simply. Get rid of unnecessary things. . . . God's answer to materialism is a basis of Christian living that lifts above material things (p. 40).

Claim from God humility, patience, courage, faith and love (p. 43).

Egoism or pride is one of our greatest enemies (p. 48).

When you bury a sin, don't visit the grave too often (p. 49).

I must let Christ run my life—always self before. Release from fear, timidity, inferiority (p. 53).

Beatitudes: Poor in spirit—the separated; those who mourn (feel world's sorrow); the meek who inherit; hunger and thirst after righteousness (after surrender, not self-righteousness); are merciful (merciful to sins of others), Mercy and righteousness make pure in heart. Peacemakers (p. 60) [Matthew 5:2-12].

Start the person on a new life with simple, concrete and definite suggestions, regarding Bible study, prayer, overcoming temptation and service for others (p. 14).

The strength of a man's decision is his willingness to be held to it. Stretched as God wants me to be stretched—consistent living, discipline, no letting down, no retiring age, a life spent in action. The proportion—thinking and living for other people (p. 24).

Never let your zeal flag; maintain the spiritual glow: Rom. 12:11.[104]

[104] Moffatt Translation. The King James Version of Romans 12:11 reads: "Not slothful in business; fervent in spirit; serving the Lord;"

3

The Books That Anne Read and Recommended

Anne recommended a large number of books for spiritual growth (pp. 16 and 48). She said she felt these should be part of a Christian's diet. She also devoted four entire pages to Toyohiko Kagawa and to Kagawa's *Love: The Law of Life*, which both she and Dr. Bob had read (pp. 13, 18-20).[1] This book is still in the possession of Dr. Bob's family. As we mention in a moment, Anne discussed, at page 46 of her Journal, an early book by Sam Shoemaker; and she quoted E. Stanley Jones at page 48, having earlier recommended *all* of the Jones books for spiritual reading. And that is enough for our preliminaries. Except, we hasten to point out, that the Bible was, with Anne, as it was with Dr. Bob and the pioneers, number one on her recommended reading list.

One A.A. historian believes Dr. Bob had a "required reading list."[2] As the footnote shows, we do not agree. And the supposed

---

[1] Toyohiko Kagawa, *Love: The Law of Life* (Philadelphia: The John C. Winston Company, 1929).

[2] See Bill Pittman, *AA The Way It Began* (Seattle, Washington: Glen Abbey Books, 1988), p. 197. As our own research has progressed, we have become convinced there was no such list. For one thing, Dr. Bob's daughter so stated to us. For another, A.A. Conference Approved literature makes it clear that Bob did not push his books on (continued...)

list mentions only five books. It does, however, appropriate list the Bible as number one on that list, and Anne did write at pages 16 and 48:

> Of course the Bible ought to be the main Source Book of all. No day ought to pass without reading it. Read until some passage comes that "hits" you. Then pause and meditate over its meaning for your life. Begin reading the Bible with the Book of Acts and follow up with the Gospels and then the Epistles of Paul. Let "Revelation" alone for a while. The Psalms ought to be read and the Prophets.

Dr. Bob agreed with Anne about the Bible's importance. He read it—cover to cover—three times. He read it nightly; and studied a familiar verse every morning.[3] He said the early AA's "were convinced that the answer to their problems was in the Good Book."[4] The Bible was stressed as reading material in the early A.A. recovery program.[5] And Dr. Bob frequently quoted passages from it.[6]

Anne held the Oxford Group view that God should, could, and would guide reading. She felt other guided people could help with such guidance. She wrote:

---

[2] (...continued)
anyone. And, finally, the number of books he recommended and favored for reading far exceeded the few books on the supposed "required" list. We therefore believe this is just another case where "more will be revealed" as we learn more and more about Dr. Bob, Anne, and their spiritual program. See Dick B., *Dr. Bob's Library: Books for Twelve Step Growth*, rev. Paradise ed. (San Rafael, CA: Paradise Research Publications, 1994), p. xi, *et seq*.

[3] See Dick B., *Dr. Bob's Library: Books for Twelve Step Growth* (CA: Paradise Research Publications, 1994), pp. 13-14.

[4] *DR. BOB and the Good Oldtimers* (New York: A.A. World Services, Inc., 1980), p. 96.

[5] *DR. BOB*, pp. 150-51.

[6] *DR. BOB*, pp. 314, 310.

> *Let all your reading be guided.* What does God want me to read? A newly surrendered person is like a convalescent after an operation. He needs a carefully balanced diet of nourishing and easily assimilated food. Reading is an essential part of the Christian's diet. It is important that he read that which can be assimilated and will be nourishing. If you do not know what books to read see some one who is surrendered and who is mature in the Groups (p. 16, italics in original).

Then she was specific. She suggested, "Biographies, or stories of changed lives are very helpful for the young Christian" (p. 16). And she listed the following Oxford Group titles in that category:

1. *Life Changers* by Begbie.[7]
2. *Children of the Second Birth* by Shoemaker.[8]
3. *New Lives for Old* by Reynolds.[9]
4. *For Sinners Only* by Russell.[10]
5. *Twice-Born Men* by Begbie.[11]
6. *Twice-Born Ministers* by Shoemaker.[12]

Dr. Bob's family still owns copies of most of these books, or has donated copies to Dr. Bob's Home in Akron, Ohio. Dr. Bob is known to have read them all.[13]

Next, Anne recommended these popular titles:

---

[7] Harold Begbie, *Life Changers* (London: Mills & Boon, Ltd., 1932).

[8] Samuel M. Shoemaker, Jr., *Children of the Second Birth* (New York: Fleming H. Revell, 1927).

[9] Amelia S. Reynolds, *New Lives for Old* (New York: Fleming H. Revell, 1929).

[10] A. J. Russell, *For Sinners Only* (London: Hodder & Stoughton, 1932).

[11] Harold Begbie, *Twice-Born Men* (New York: Fleming H. Revell, 1909).

[12] Samuel M. Shoemaker, *Twice-Born Ministers* (New York: Fleming H. Revell, 1929).

[13] See Dick B., *Dr. Bob's Library*, pp. 20-21.

1. *He That Cometh* by Oxford Group writer Geoffrey Allen.[14]
2. *The Conversion of the Church* by Shoemaker.[15]
3. "All of E. Stanley Jones' books are very good."[16]
4. *The Meaning of Prayer* and *The Manhood of the Master* by Fosdick.[17]

Anne took special note of Dr. Shoemaker's *If I Be Lifted Up*.[18] She said, "An understanding of the Cross and its meaning for life is absolutely essential. The best popular interpretation I know is, 'If I be Lifted Up', Shoemaker. It is a group of lenten sermons. Christ ought to be as real to us as our nearest and best friend" (p. 16).

Finally, Anne had these recommendations on the life of Christ: She said, "One should by all means read at least one book on the life of Christ a year for a while. More would be better" (p. 16). She said the following "are all good":

[14] Geoffrey Allen, *He That Cometh* (New York: The Macmillan Company, 1933). This book was also on Sam Shoemaker's *Evangel* list of recommended Oxford Group literature.

[15] Samuel M. Shoemaker, *The Conversion of the Church* (New York: Fleming H. Revell, 1932). This book also was on *The Evangel* Oxford Group literature list.

[16] For some of the best known Jones books, see E. Stanley Jones, *Christ at the Round Table* (New York: The Abingdon Press, 1928); *The Christ of Every Road* (New York: The Abingdon Press, 1930); *The Christ of the Mount* (New York: The Abingdon Press, 1930)—Dr. Bob's family still owns a copy; *The Christ of the Indian Road* (New York: The Abingdon Press, 1925); *Christ and Human Suffering* (New York: The Abingdon Press, 1930); *Victorious Living* (New York: The Abingdon Press, 1936); *The Choice Before Us* (New York: The Abingdon Press, 1937); *Along the Indian Road* (New York: The Abingdon Press, 1939). See also Dick B., *Dr. Bob's Library*, pp. 36, 37, 64-66.

[17] Harry Emerson Fosdick, *The Meaning of Prayer* (New York: Association Press, 1926); *The Manhood of the Master* (London: Student Christian Movement, 1924). Dr. Bob read a good many Fosdick books.

[18] Samuel M. Shoemaker, *If I Be Lifted Up* (Mew York: Fleming H. Revell, 1931).

1. *The Life of Jesus Christ* by Stalker.[19]
2. *Jesus of Nazareth* by Barton.[20]
3. *The Jesus of History* by Glover.[21]
4. *The Man Christ Jesus* by Speer.[22]

She added emphatically, "See your ministers for others if you desire. But get those biographies of the Master which bring out his humanity" (p. 16).

Anne said much about Toyohiko Kagawa's books. As to Kagawa's views on truth and the faults of others, Anne wrote:

> Though I myself do not have the memory of having told a lie, I think myself innocent, yet when anyone else commits robbery . . . I must ask forgiveness of God for it. The Jesus who thought like that was truly the King of Truth. The Kingship of Truth becomes God-consciousness. One bears the fault of others on his shoulders and asks forgiveness of God for them, as if they were his own. . . . Students and learned men who have never undertaken to bear the consequences of the failures of others find it impossible to grasp this (p. 13).

Then, as to Kagawa on saving and serving others, she wrote:

> The moment we ourselves are saved, we must set ourselves to saving others. The way Christ became the Atoning Lamb was by his hanging on the Cross and dying there. And Christianity for me means to dedicate myself to serve others even unto death. That, I am convinced, is the true way of Jesus Christ. Christianity means to save others. That is the way of the Cross, and the true way of Christ (p. 13).

---

[19] Rev. James Stalker, *The Life of Jesus Christ* (New York: Fleming H. Revell, 1891).

[20] George A. Barton, *Jesus of Nazareth: A Biography* (New York: The Macmillan Company, 1922).

[21] T. R. Glover, *The Jesus of History* (New York: Association Press, 1919).

[22] Robert E. Speer, *Studies of the Man Christ Jesus* (New York: Fleming H. Revell, 1896).

Finally, as to Kagawa's remarks on loving men to the uttermost:

> To love men to the uttermost—that is what Christ does. To that end, sin must be redeemed. . . . To turn blind eyes and deaf ears toward these [prostitutes, unemployed, slum conditions] this is sin! Christ was fully conscious of such conditions. . . . He thought as God does about them, he suffered profoundly in his soul about them, and so was put on the Cross and died (p. 13).

Anne was truly attempting to grasp the meaning of Christian love, forgiveness, witness, and service. Her remarks foreshadowed Dr. Bob's later observation that A.A.'s Twelve Steps—which he said were based on the philosophy of the Sermon on the Mount—could be simmered to their essence as Love and Service.[23]

Anne devoted three more pages to Kagawa's views on love. On page 19, she wrote:

> Christ's basic principle, which he expressed in saying that we must love even the very least of them . . . grew out of the fact that he had entered into the consciousness of God. The consciousness of atonement, that is, the conscious sharing of the atoning purposes of God.

On page 20:

> The purpose of our having mystical experience is not that we may achieve our own personal satisfaction, but that we may succor the poor, help those who are in trouble, and educate the masses.

And on page 21:

> It may be that from the standpoint of criminology, criminals are physiologically different from other men, and cannot become better men. But from Christ's standpoint, they can be saved. The reason that prayer meetings have grown musty is because we have

---

[23] *DR. BOB*, pp. 338, 228.

> ceased to believe in the power of God which can save. We do not sincerely believe in prayer.
>
> . . . Christ must enter more deeply into our experience, and we must pray with deep conviction. Is it not written that prayer is inevitably answered? Christ went through with his death upon the Cross courageously because he believed that salvation could be made complete. . . . We must pray with faith, though others may think us superstitious.

This is just a taste of the lady of faith, courage, and love of whom we wrote in the first chapter!

In 1923, Sam Shoemaker wrote a little book that was published by the International Committee of the Young Men's Christian Association. It was titled *One Boy's Influence.*[24] And it was the story of Dr. Shoemaker's meeting a young man on a train from Chicago. It told how Sam shared his experience with the young man and brought him to a decision for Christ. The young man, in turn, was interested in helping others to change to a better life; and Shoemaker told of the methods the young man used, the influence that he had, and the life-changes that occurred through his work. Anne read this book and discussed part of it at pages 46 and 47 of her Journal. She wrote:

> One thing you will not do, and that is, not to witness beyond your experience. Sam Shoemaker in his little book, "One Boy's Influence," says, "There are two directions in which a man's mind must be continually travelling if he was to be successful and useful as a Christian—one upwards toward God, the other is out towards men." Then he goes on to tell this young man who is but a recently surrendered lad that *the only key to religion is to give it away; it will increase as you give it* (emphasis added).

---

[24] Shoemaker, Jr., *One Boy's Influence*, *supra.*

This appears to be one of the earliest recitals of the A.A. adage: "You have to give it away to keep it"—a principle which Sam Shoemaker often espoused.[25]

[25] *Alcoholics Anonymous*, 2d ed., p. 341: "We GIVE AWAY TO KEEP. . . . We've got to continue to give it away in order to keep it."

4

Anne's Discussion of Twenty-eight Oxford Group Concepts

The decision to discuss Oxford Group principles and practices in terms of twenty-eight concepts we believe influenced A.A. is the result of the author's research. Anne did not approach them in that way. Nor did Oxford Group writers.

For example, *What Is The Oxford Group?* discussed four points, which it said were the keys to the kind of spiritual life God wishes us to lead—Absolute Honesty, Absolute Purity, Absolute Unselfishness, and Absolute Love.[1] And it listed four practical spiritual activities to be spiritually reborn and by which we should live in the state in which the four absolutes are guides to a life in God—(1) Sharing of sins and as Witness; (2) Surrender; (3)

---

[1] See The Layman with a Notebook, *What Is The Oxford Group?* (London: Oxford University Press, 1933), pp. 7, 73-118. These are the Four Absolutes, or Four Standards, the Oxford Group used and which were frequently referred to by Dr. Bob and Bill W. See *DR. BOB and the Good Oldtimers* (New York: A.A. World Services, Inc., 1980), pp. 54, 163; *Pass It On* (New York: A.A. World Services, Inc., 1984), pp. 114, 127, 172; *Alcoholics Anonymous Comes of Age*, (New York: A.A. World Services, Inc., 1979), pp. 75, 161; *The Language of the Heart* (New York: The A.A. Grapevine, Inc., 1988), pp. 196-200; *The Co-Founders of Alcoholics Anonymous; Biographical Sketches; Their Last Major Talks* (8th Printing, New York: A.A. World Services, Inc., 1972, 1975), pp. 12-14; *Lois Remembers* (New York: Al-Anon Family Group Headquarters, 1987), p. 92.

Restitution; and (4) Listening to, accepting, and relying on God's Guidance.[2]

The Eight Points of the Oxford Group discussed eight Oxford Group points—God's Plan, Confession, Restitution, Four Absolutes, Quiet Time, Guidance, Life-changing, and Fellowship.[3] And Sherwood Sunderland Day's *The Principles of the Group* discussed seven Oxford Group "principles of the Bible"—God-Guidance, Fearless Dealing with Sin, Sharing, The Necessity for Adequate Intelligent Expressional Activity, Stewardship, Team-Work, and Loyalty.[4]

From these and other Oxford Group and Shoemaker books, we have constructed and listed twenty-eight concepts which, though appearing to overlap each other, each state an Oxford Group idea, belief, practice, or principle we believe influenced A.A.

Anne discussed each of the twenty-eight principles in her Journal. Long-time Oxford Group activists, Garth Lean, Michael Hutchinson, James and Eleanor Newton, and Willard Hunter confirmed to the author that the twenty-eight concepts are valid Oxford Group concepts. Similarly, Mrs. W. Irving Harris (long-time Oxford Group member, good friend of Bill Wilson, and widow of Sam Shoemaker's assistant minister and biographer, Rev. W. Irving Harris) confirmed to the author the validity of the concepts, as far as Shoemaker's views were concerned.

For documentation as to where and how the twenty-eight concepts can be found in the Bible, the Oxford Group itself,

---

[2] See *What Is The Oxford Group?*, pp. 8, 9, 25-72. And see, for comparison, *DR. BOB*, pp. 57, 92, 75, 86; *AA Comes of Age*, p. 39; Big Book, p. xvi; *The Language of the Heart*, pp. 196, 298; *Lois Remembers*, p. 92.

[3] Clarence Irving Benson, *The Eight Points of the Oxford Group* (London: Oxford University Press, 1936).

[4] Sherwood Sunderland Day, *The Principles of the Group* (Pamphlet published by The Oxford Group and printed in Great Britain at the University Press, Oxford, by John Johnson, Printer to the University, no date). See also Irving Harris, *The Breeze of the Spirit* (New York: The Seabury Press, 1978), pp. 18-21; and Dick B., *New Light on Alcoholism: The A.A. Legacy from Sam Shoemaker* (CA: Good Book Publishing Co., 1994), pp. 68-72.

Shoemaker's writings, and A.A. literature, see the Appendix in our book. In this chapter, we will simply list the concepts and briefly quote Anne's statements about them.

God

The Oxford Group spoke of God as He is described in the Bible—Creator, Almighty, Jehovah [Lord], Father, Love, and Spirit. So did Anne. She wrote of God as Love (pp. 23, 42, 44); Spirit (pp. 8, 23, 27, 32, 37, 44, 51, 50, 58); Lord (pp. 24, 26, 51); Father (pp. 11, 58); King (p. 13); and Power (pp. 47, 61).

For example, she wrote: "What things in me make the Holy Spirit unwilling to use me" (p. 50)? "[T]he Holy Spirit is the leader and dictator of this group" (p. 50). "The Holy Spirit is ready to dictate a perfect plan" (p. 29). "A person can't ooze into the Kingdom of God" (p. 49). "Seek ye first the Kingdom of God" (p. 39). She spoke of "the guidance of the Holy Spirit" (p. 29), the "power of the Holy Spirit" (p. 44), the "direction of the Holy Spirit" (p. 22), and being "in touch with the Holy Spirit" (p. 26). She spoke of being "in touch with God" (p. 25). She paraphrased 2 Peter 1:21 that all Scripture was written by "holy men of God [who] spake *as they* were moved by the Holy Ghost" (p. 23). She spoke of "the atoning purposes of God" (p. 19). She called "God the universal provider, the ally, the tame confederate" (p. 23). She often contrasted God with the Devil or Satan (pp. 14, 25, 47).

Some seventeen years after A.A. was founded, Bill Wilson chose to write, in *Twelve Steps and Twelve Traditions*, "You can, if you wish, make A.A. itself your higher power."[5] But that was not an Oxford Group concept. Anne, in contrast, discussed what she called such "Funk Holes." She wrote:

> Unwillingness to use the word Christ. Talking about a house party without saying anything about your own personal defeats and how

---

[5] *Twelve Steps and Twelve Traditions* (New York: A.A. World Services, Inc., 1953), p. 27.

you faced up to Jesus Christ. Using the word "Group" instead of "Christ" (p. 15).

God Has a Plan

Dr. Frank Buchman, the Oxford Group Founder, frequently spoke about "God's Plan."[6] So did Reverend Sam Shoemaker, the New York Oxford Group leader.[7] Early AA's picked up on this concept.[8] And Anne wrote:

> One of the necessities for leadership is that we be sensitive to what God's plan is, not rigid in our own ideas and interpreting what we think is God's plan, but looking continuously for what His real plan is, for ourselves, for our families, or for somebody else. The secret lies in always keeping one ear to the Holy Spirit (p. 37).

Man's Chief End—Harmonizing His Life with God's Plan

Oxford Group Theologian B. H. Streeter wrote:

> The only sensible course for the individual is to ask what is God's Plan for him, and then endeavor to carry out that plan. For if we can discern anything of God's Plan for us, common sense demands that we give ourselves entirely to it.[9]

Shoemaker wrote, "If we look after God's Plan, He takes care of our needs."[10] Dr. Bob's Big Book story underlined the idea,

---

[6] Frank N. D. Buchman, *Remaking the World* (London: Blandford Press, 1961), pp. 53, 61, 63, 77.

[7] Samuel M. Shoemaker, *National Awakening* (NY: Harper & Brothers, 1936), p. 41; *Children of the Second Birth* (New York: Fleming H. Revell, 1927), p. 27; *Religion That Works* (New York: Fleming H. Revell, 1928), p. 19.

[8] *DR. BOB*, p. 145; *Lois Remembers*, p. 100. Compare Big Book, p. 237.

[9] B. H. Streeter, *The God Who Speaks* (New York: Macmillan, 1936), p. 17.

[10] Shoemaker, *National Awakening*, p. 42, citing Matthew 6:32-33.

stating, "Your Heavenly Father will never let you down!" (p. 181).[11] Anne wrote:

> Keep Divine Perspective in mind. Get a proper perspective of your own task. "You have not chosen me, but I have chosen you." Complete abandonment of self to God. God has work He wants done, and our will can block it (p. 38).

Belief in God

Oxford Group scholar Philip Leon wrote, "The facts with which I propose to start here as undeniable are God and myself."[12] Proposing an experiment for achieving security through faith in God, Shoemaker said we must first believe that God IS.[13] And these Oxford Group writers cited Hebrews 11:6 in support:

> But without faith *it is* impossible to please *him* [God]; for he that cometh to God must believe that he is, and *that* he is a rewarder of them that diligently seek him.[14]

The Big Book said, "God either is, or He isn't" (p. 53). Anne spoke about "people who don't feel in touch with God." She said:

> It is not enough to surrender sin, but we must also claim the victory of the resurrection life. It is God that does it. Nothing you can do is of any use (p. 30).

---

[11] See also Big Book, p 164; and p. 77, the latter stating, "Our real purpose is to fit ourselves to be of maximum service to God and the people about us." The Eleventh Step speaks of "praying only for knowledge of His will for us and the power to carry that out" (p. 59).

[12] Philip Leon, *The Philosophy of Courage or The Oxford Group Way* (New York: Oxford University Press, 1939), p. 19.

[13] Shoemaker, *National Awakening*, p. 40.

[14] See Samuel M. Shoemaker, *The Gospel According to You* (New York: Fleming H. Revell, 1934), p. 47; Leslie D. Weatherhead, *How Can I Find God?* (New York: Fleming H. Revell, 1934), p. 89; Harold Begbie, *The Day That Changed the World* (New York: Hodder & Stoughton, 1913), p. 211.

Sin

The Oxford Group took a very practical view of sin and its reality. Frank Buchman wrote:

> I don't know if you believe in sin or not, but it is here. Don't spend the rest of the day arguing if it exists or not.[15]

Harold Begbie quoted Buchman on sin: "It isn't any intellectual difficulty which is keeping you from God. It is sin."[16] A. J. Russell quoted Buchman on sin and added his own definition, saying:

> Sin was anything done contrary to the Will of God, as shown by the New Testament or by direct guidance. . . . The best definition of sin that we have is that sin is anything in my life which keeps me from God and from other people.[17]

Dr. Shoemaker accepted these definitions, but used language a bit more familiar to AAs:

> Sin is the thing that keeps us from being channels of God's power. Whatever keeps us from a living, loving relation with other people—or from a vital and open relationship with God is sin.[18]

> I had brought out into the open a number of what we old-fashionedly called "sins," which were blocking me from communion with God.[19]

---

[15] Buchman, *Remaking the World*, p. 54.

[16] Harold Begbie, *Life Changers* (London: Mills & Boon, Ltd., 1932), p. 14.

[17] A. J. Russell, *For Sinners Only* (London: Hodder & Stoughton, 1932), pp. 61, 319.

[18] Samuel M. Shoemaker, *How to Become a Christian* (New York: Harper & Brothers, 1953), p. 56.

[19] Samuel M. Shoemaker, *Twice-Born Ministers* (New York: Fleming H. Revell, 1929), p. 30.

> But if sin be looked upon as anything that puts a barrier between us and Christ, or between us and other people, then there are many things which we must call by the name of sin.[20]

So Oxford Group adherents were speaking of sin as behavior that "keeps" one from God and others, that "blocks" from communion with God, and that puts "barriers" between us and God and other people.

One will search long and hard for the word "sin" in A.A. today; but it was part and parcel of the description of "defects," "shortcomings," and "sins" in A.A.'s first two of its original six steps.[21] And the idea that character defects and shortcomings *block* one from God is still very present in the language of the Big Book at pages 64 and 71.

What did Anne have to say? These are some of her remarks:

> Is there anything in us which blocks God? Work, it matters to God. Sin isn't merely inconvenience. It is serious business (p. 38).

> Obedience is one of the key-words of the Christian Life. Refusal to obey blocks the channel, and prevents further word from God (p. 16).

Surrender

Oxford Group Founder Frank Buchman wrote:

> By a miracle of the Spirit, God can speak to every man. . . . When man listens, God speaks. When man obeys, God acts. . . . Accurate, adequate information can come from the Mind of God to the minds of men who are willing to take their orders from Him.[22]

---

[20] Samuel M. Shoemaker, *They're on the Way* (New York: E. P. Dutton & Co., 1951), p. 154. *Cf.*, 1 John 3:4: ". . . sin is the transgression of the law."

[21] *Pass It On*, p. 197.

[22] Buchman, *Remaking the World*, p. 42.

What Is The Oxford Group? defined surrender as follows:

> Surrender to God is our actual passing from a life of Sin to a life God-Guided and Christ-conscious. . . . It is the giving up of our old ineffective spiritual lives and taking on a life of spiritual activity in everything we do or say. . . . Surrender is our complete severance from our old self and endeavoring to live by God's Guidance as one with Christ. . . . Surrendering our lives to God means a complete giving back to God of the will-power He gave us at Creation (p. 41).

The Eight Points of the Oxford Group asked if there were a technique of finding one's life plan? "There is," it answered, and said:

> The initial step and the indispensable step in the quest is *absolute surrender of our lives to God* [italics in original]. All that is in self, good, bad, and indifferent, must be handed over to God (p. 17).

Sam Shoemaker wrote:

> Surrender of the whole self to God means the complete dedication, by deliberate act of the will, of one's entire personality to doing the will of God so far as we can discover it.[23]

The history of early Akron A.A. is replete with stories about the AAs' surrenders to God.[24] The Big Book's discussion of Step Three, from pages 60 to 64, is filled with language from the foregoing writings. It says on page 60, "we decided to turn our will and our life over to God as we understood Him." Then, on page 62, "Next, we decided that hereafter in this drama of life, God was going to be our Director." Then on page 63, the so-called Third Step Prayer, ending, "May I do Thy will always!"

---

[23] Samuel M. Shoemaker, *Realizing Religion* (New York: Association Press, 1923), p. 29.

[24] *DR. BOB*, pp. 89, 92, 93, 110; *Pass It On*, p. 198 (the original 7th Step).

Anne wrote extensively on Surrender. On page 42, she said:

> Surrender is a complete handing over of our wills to God, a reckless abandon of ourselves, all that we have, all that we think, that we are, everything we hold dear, to God to do what He likes with, to maintain an attitude of willingness to accept in child-wants and for those things He brings us in touch with.

On pages 4 and 56, Anne used a common Oxford Group expression: "Surrender of as much of himself as he knows to as much of God as he knows."[25] She spoke repeatedly of surrendering self-will, anger, resentment, pride, fear, dishonesty, sins, and wills (pp. 17, 18, 25, 37, 43, 61, 62).

Life-Change

Harold Begbie wrote a book about Oxford Group Founder Frank Buchman's approach, and the title was *Life Changers*. And *The Eight Points of the Oxford Group* said the following about life-changing:

> Absolute surrender includes all that the New Testament means by converting. It is conversion with a definite programme of world changing through life changing. The Group is insistent that every Christian be a life changer. The New Testament knows nothing of a self-contained conversion (p. 158).

Shoemaker wrote in *The Church Can Save the World*:

> We need steady life-changing as the main drive of our work. The spiritual front is not alone a show of conviction, it is a force of persuasion. We need to know how to recognize sin, how to get it

[25] Stephen Foot, *Life Began Yesterday* (New York: Harper & Brothers, 1935), p. 175: "That is surrender. Surrender of all one knows of self to all one knows of God."

> shared, surrendered, forgiven, restored for, and then used to help others in like case.[26]

Anne wrote no less enthusiastically on this point. On page 23, she spoke of "Lifechanging" as a principal motive for leadership. On page 27, she wrote, "That the axis of this group is the changed life. That the witness is related to the people there." This brings to our mind A.A.'s 5th Tradition: "Each group has but one primary purpose—to carry its message to the alcoholic who still suffers."

Soul Surgery

Howard A. Walter wrote a book titled *Soul Surgery* to describe Frank Buchman's "art" of changing lives.[27] Dr. Bob owned, studied, and loaned to others this basic Oxford Group book. It was devoted to personal evangelism but dwelt on Frank Buchman's Five C's: (1) Confidence, (2) Confession, (3) Conviction, (4) Conversion, and (5) Conservation (sometimes called Continuance). We believe these "procedures" became the basis for most of A.A.'s Steps. The term "soul surgery" was part of the working language of early A.A. Thus *DR. BOB* spoke of "No pay for soul surgery" (p. 54). A.A. historian Dr. Ernest Kurtz reported that both Lois Wilson (Bill's wife) and Henrietta Seiberling had an aversion to the term.[28] However, Buchman's Five C's were spoken of with frequency by AAs.[29]

---

[26] Samuel M. Shoemaker, *The Church Can Save the World* (New York: Harper & Brothers, 1938), p. 153.

[27] Howard A. Walter, *Soul Surgery: Some Thoughts on Incisive Personal Work* (Calcutta, India: Association Press, 1919).

[28] Ernest Kurtz, *Not-God*, exp. ed. (MN: Hazelden, 1991), pp. 49, 228.

[29] See, for example, Richmond Walker, *For Drunks Only: One Man's Reaction to Alcoholics Anonymous* (Published in 1945; Reprinted by Hazelden), pp. 45-46; *The 7 Points of Alcoholics Anonymous*, rev. ed. (Seattle: Glen Abbey Books, 1989), pp. 91-93. See also Kurtz, *Not-God*, pp. 48-49.

Shoemaker wrote about the Five C's in his first book, *Realizing Religion*, saying as to the curing of sick souls:

> And how do you do it? It may help to keep our object in view if we choose five words which will cover the usual stages of development: "Confidence; Confession; Conviction; Conversion; Conservation." You may feel this is a bit formidable. But for these words I am indebted to Frank N. D. Buchman (pp. 79-80).[30]

Anne devoted all of page 4 of her Journal to the Five C's.

On "Confidence" she wrote, "Get a person to talk about his interests. . . . Learn to intrigue people with stories of individual lives that have been changed." On "Confession" she wrote, "You must share deeply with him, *under guidance*; You may be guided to share your deepest sin, and this will clear the way for him to share his." On "Conviction" she wrote, "Try to bring a person to a decision to 'surrender as much of himself as he knows to as much of God as he knows.'" On "Conversion" she wrote, "This is the turning to God, the decision, the surrender." On "Continuance" she wrote, "Stay with the newly surrendered person until he grows up and becomes a life-changer" (italics in original).

Decision

Philip Brown pointed out that the great venture of faith, of finding God—the surrender that leads to a religious experience—starts with a *decision*.[31] Shoemaker wrote in *The Conversion of the Church*:

---

[30] See also Shoemaker, *Twice-Born Ministers*, p. 93, for a discussion of the "difficult art of soul-surgery."

[31] Philip M. Brown, *The Venture of Belief* (NY: Fleming H. Revell, 1935), pp. 26-28. See also Henry Wright, *The Will of God and a Man's Lifework* (New York: The Young Men's Christian Association, 1909), which contains an entire chapter titled, "The Decision to Do God's Will" (pp. 43-114). Wright was the person who was said most to have influenced Frank Buchman's ideas. See Rev. T. Willard Hunter, *World-Changing Through Life-Changing* (Thesis, Andover-Newton Theological School, 1977), pp. 15-16.

> Of course, the mere externalizing of these difficulties does not banish them. They must be gathered up in a new decision of the will and handed over to God in a new surrender—this step of decision.[32]

The Big Book starts A.A.'s action steps with a *decision*. Step Three says, "Made a decision to turn our will and our lives over to the care of God *as we understood Him*" (p. 59). It continues, "Being convinced, *we were at Step Three*, which is that we decided to turn our will and our life over to God as we understood Him" (p. 60).

In Chapter Two, we covered Anne's remarks about "decision;" and we simply point out here that, when she spoke of "conversion," she said, "This is the . . . the decision" (p. 4). This concept also appears at pages 37, 42, and 51 of her Journal.

Self-Examination

Henry Drummond, whose ideas greatly influenced the Oxford Group, said that willingness to do God's will had to commence with man's "in-look." He said man needs to "devote his soul to self-examination, to self examination of the most solemn and searching kind."[33] Drummond suggested making the "moral test."[34] And Frank Buchman suggested that the root problems to look for were resentment, selfishness, dishonesty, and fear.[35] In *How to Become a Christian*, Shoemaker wrote:

> One of the simplest and best rules for self-examination that I know is to use the Four Standards which Dr. Robert E. Speer said

---

[32] Samuel M. Shoemaker, *The Conversion of the Church* (New York: Fleming H. Revell, 1932), p. 39.

[33] Henry Drummond, *The Ideal Life* (New York: Hodder & Stoughton, 1897), p. 316.

[34] Walter, *Soul Surgery*, so quotes Drummond, at page 49.

[35] Buchman, *Remaking the World*, pp. 24, 28, 38.

> represented the summary of the Sermon on the Mount—Absolute Honesty, Absolute Purity, Absolute Unselfishness, and Absolute Love. Review your life in their light. Put down everything that doesn't measure up (pp. 56-67).

A.A.'s Fourth Step requires, ". . . a searching and fearless moral inventory of ourselves" (p. 59). It suggests listing resentments, fears, selfish sex conduct, and harms (pp. 64-71). And the lists suggest that possible dishonesty will be unearthed.

In an early part of her Journal, Anne had suggested the "moral test" (p. 4, 14). She covered examination of self, and for resentment, fear, and dishonesty (pp. 18-19, 25, 32, 36-37, 45). The Big Book plainly states that its moral inventory ideas came from the Oxford Group (p. xvi). And Bill W. himself acknowledged, in *AA Comes of Age*, that A.A. got its idea of self-examination from the Oxford Group via Shoemaker (p. 39).

Confession

Oxford Group writers consistently wrote of James 5:16 when they spoke of Sharing by Confession. James 5:16 reads, "Confess *your* faults one to another, and pray for one another, that ye may be healed." *What Is The Oxford Group?* cited this verse and said:

> Sharing of sins as practiced by the Oxford Group is sharing in the ordinary sense of the word; in plain language it is telling or talking over, our sins with another whose life has already been surrendered to God (p. 27).

Shoemaker quoted and discussed James 5:16 in *The Conversion of the Church* at page 35. So did A.A.'s *Pass It On* at page 128. So did Anne in her Journal at page 32. And the Big Book, at page xvi, and *Lois Remembers*, at page 92, make clear the Oxford Group origins of the Fifth Step confession. Bill recalled Anne's reading to him and Dr. Bob from the Bible and said, "James [the

Book of James in the Bible] was our favorite."[36] Dr. Bob himself specified the Book of James as "absolutely essential."[37]

As our Fifth Step discussion in Chapter Two showed, Anne's Journal covered all these Sharing-by-Confession ideas.

Conviction

This is an unfamiliar word in modern A.A. But it had great meaning for the Oxford Group, Sam Shoemaker, and Anne Smith. It was one of the Five C's, of which A.A. did speak. Oxford Group writer Olive Jones provided this definition: "*Conviction*, by which we come to the conscious realization of our sins which shut God away from us."[38] Harold Begbie wrote in *Life Changers*:

> The third, conviction of sin, is the normal result of the impact upon a man of a quality of life which he instinctively knows to be superior to his own, the lack of which he recognizes as an offense against God, and as his fault and only his (p. 169).

Frank Buchman's mentor, Dwight Moody, wrote that "being convicted of sin" means consciousness of wrongdoing—finding out that you are lost.[39] Sam Shoemaker wrote in *Realizing Religion*:

> It was consciousness of personal sin which drew from my friend those pathetic and tremendously healthy words: Oh! to be made over in the Spirit! I want a rebirth, but it comes not in one agony. Oh! how I want freedom from these deadening doubts, from this horrible, haunting sense, no "knowledge," of sin—this hopeless self-hatred and suffering (p. 21).

---

[36] *DR. BOB*, p. 71.

[37] *DR. BOB*, p. 96.

[38] Olive Jones, *Inspired Children* (New York: Harper & Brothers, 1933), p. 135.

[39] William R. Moody, *The Life of D. L. Moody* (New York: Fleming H. Revell, 1900), p. 239

We believe A.A.'s Sixth Step—becoming entirely ready to have God remove all the defects of character (sins) discovered by self-examination and confession—derives from the Oxford Group "Conviction" idea.

As we have shown, Anne discussed "Conviction" in her Journal and said that each day we should see more and more things that need to be surrendered (p. 56). And she said people must be made "to face up to the thing that is their cross in life" (pp. 29-30).

What were the Oxford Group, Anne, and the Sixth Step talking about? We believe they were saying that one must acquire a strong sense from his or her own self-examination and confession, that all is not well—not well at all! That there is an urgent need for *change*; a sense that it will take the power of God to effect the change; a willingness for that change to occur; and then a seeking of God's help to bring it about.

Conversion

Oxford Group people, Sam Shoemaker, and Anne Smith frequently quoted William James's definition of conversion:

> The process, gradual or sudden, by which a self, hitherto divided and consciously wrong, inferior and unhappy becomes unified, consciously right, superior and happy.[40]

Bill Wilson wrote Dr. Carl Jung that Jung's prescription for a religious or conversion experience as the solution for alcoholism "proved to be the foundation of such success as Alcoholics Anonymous has since achieved. This made conversion experience . . . available on an almost wholesale basis."[41]

---

[40] See Shoemaker, *Realizing Religion*, p. 22; Knippel, *Samuel M. Shoemaker's Theological Influence on William G. Wilson's Twelve Step Spiritual Recovery Program*, (Dissertation, St. Louis University, 1987), p. 133; Anne Smith's Journal, p. 28.

[41] *Pass It On*, p. 383.

From this idea, we believe, developed the language of A.A.'s Seventh Step: "Humbly asked Him [God] to *remove* our shortcomings" (p. 59, italics added).

Geoffrey Allen, in a book Anne Smith recommended, said:

> To blame, or to seek to repress irritation or anxiety is merely to make it worse. . . . They fall short of the standard of fearless, spontaneous love, and as such as symptoms of sin, with which the devil may make us complacent, *but which God can remove*. The standard is clear; anything in life which keeps me from the fullness of the love of God, or which keeps me from bringing my neighbor to God, is evil, and can and must be exposed, forgiven and cured (italics added).[42]

Anne wrote at page 46 of her Journal on such sins as possessiveness, temper, self-pity, selfishness, and pride. She said, "Christ can only *remove* them and replace them with a new quality of life" (italics added). And she cited Romans 12. As we previously said, Anne wrote that conversion was the turning to God.

Conservation or Continuance

There are two aspects of Conservation. One has to do with *continuing* the life-changing surrender process through Quiet Time, Bible study, prayer, and listening for leading thoughts. The other has to do with *helping others* to whom witness is made of one's life-change. We will not here analyze the difference, but rather present a few of the Oxford Group, Sam Shoemaker, and Anne Smith statements about this fifth part of the soul-surgery art.

H. A. Walter's *Soul Surgery* said: There must be a real and developing prayer life; of equal importance the feeding of the soul "day by day on God's living Word revealed in the Scriptures;" and the all important Guidance (pp. 134-37). Frank Buchman's beliefs

---

[42] Geoffrey Allen, *He That Cometh* (New York: The Macmillan Company, 1933), p. 147.

about continued spiritual growth were described as follows by Garth Lean in *Cast Out Your Nets*:[43]

> The spiritual child's requirements are . . . simple. To grow to adulthood, he needs food, air, and exercise" (p. 101). "FOOD is primarily the Bible. 'Man shall not live by bread alone but by every word that proceeds from the mouth of God.'" (p. 102).[44] "AIR. A person must breathe in or suffocate, he must breathe out or burst. It is the same way with prayer. It should be two-way. Many people do suffocate spiritually because they breathe out, but never breathe in. They are so busy telling God what to do for them that they never listen to what He wants to do for them. . . . So be sure your spiritual child breathes in as well as out, that he gives regular and adequate time to let God speak to him" (p. 103). "EXERCISE. Jesus often gave people something to do which resulted in their growth. He sent out seventy disciples two by two with exact instructions what to do—and rejoiced on their return. At other times growth resulted, without instructions, from something he did with them. . . . Bohler's advice to [John] Wesley [was], "Preach faith till you have it; then, because you have it, you will preach faith'" (pp. 106-09).

At page 82 in *Realizing Religion*, Shoemaker stressed reading the Bible, prayer, public worship, and witness (fishing for men, as Jesus called it). Anne wrote the following on Conservation:

> Stay with the newly surrendered person until he grows up a life-changer (p. 4).

> Are you willing to take the amount of trouble to win others that Christ has taken to win you? (p. 43).

---

[43] Garth Lean, *Cast Out Your Nets* (London: Grosvenor, 1990).

[44] See Deuteronomy 8:3 and Matthew 4:4 for source of quote.

We do not go into the quiet time to get guidance but to realize a Presence and the mighty love of God. God has a plan and He will speak if I am still enough to listen (p. 43).

These are some suggested steps in continuance:

1. *Face the past for what it really was*. . . . Call it by its right name. . . .
2. *Burn all bridges behind you*. . . . [A]nchors need to be driven to prevent slipping backward.
3. *Witness to some friend who has come to you*. . . . One thing you will not do, and that is not to witness beyond your experience.
4. *Practice daily surrender*. . . . It is a continuous attitude of the new life.
5. *Daily Quiet Time*. . . . The method of holding Quiet Time varies some with each individual. All include prayer and Bible reading and study and patient listening to God.
6. *Be alert for symptoms of let down*. . . . Lean on Christ, not on yourself. . . . This feeling is the grip of the old life seeking to hold you, or if you prefer, The Devil fighting to keep you for his own.
7. *Blocks to guidance*. Lack of surrender; preconceived ideas of what God will or will not have us do; unwillingness to follow guidance once it is received; inadequate Quiet Time; inadequate sharing.
8. *Let all your reading be guided*. . . .
9. *Let friendships and relationships with others be guided*. Quite often one cannot break with old associations entirely. . . . God may want to use us as the means of changing those lives.
10. *Unite with a fellowship of kindred souls*. . . . You want to unite with those whose sole aim is to do the will of God and to be used of Him to change lives.
11. *Don't try, but trust*. . . . We find release not by our own efforts but by what Christ does for us and in us when we open every area of our lives to Him.

> 12. *This quality of life is an adventure not an arrival.* We surrender to God from more to more and from more to maximum. . . . Check your life constantly by the four absolutes (pp. 46-49; italics in original).

What a lady! One could take the foregoing twelve points and find a great deal that was later written in A.A.'s Big Book. And small wonder Bill W. was prompted to insert the following in Chapter Five of the Big Book:

> Many of us exclaimed [as to the Twelve Steps in the Big Book], "What an order! I can't go through with it." Do not be discouraged. No one among us has been able to maintain anything like perfect adherence to these principles. We are not saints. The point is, that we are willing to grow along spiritual lines. The principles we have set down are guides to progress. We claim spiritual progress rather than spiritual perfection (p. 60).

Bill Wilson chafed at what he considered the rigid ideals of the Oxford Group; and *Pass It On* listed eight reasons Bill later gave for rejecting many Oxford Group precepts (pp. 172-73).[45] On the other hand, Bill's wife, Lois, said the "Oxford Group kind of kicked us out," and that she and Bill were not considered "maximum" by the Oxford Group people.[46] In fact, *Lois Wilson once confided* to A.A. historian Dr. Ernest Kurtz, "*Well, I didn't have much use for the Oxford Group; I didn't think I needed conversion*" (emphasis added).[47]

---

[45] See also *AA Comes of Age*, pp. 74-75.

[46] *Pass It On*, p. 174; see also *Lois Remembers*, p. 103.

[47] Kurtz, *Not-God*, p. 218, note 58. In *Lois Remembers*, Bill's wife tells it somewhat differently. She said: "It was an ecstatic time for us both. With Ebby and another alcoholic. . . we constantly went to Oxford Group meetings. . . . I shared Bill's gratitude for what the group had done for him and for so many other people. . . . Alcoholics Anonymous (yet to be formed at that time) owes a great debt to the Oxford Group. . . . God, through the Oxford Group, had accomplished in a twinkling what I had failed to do in seventeen years. . . . I have come to see that even well-intentioned good deeds

(continued...)

Whatever the real joint Wilson opinion might have been, Dr. Bob clearly took a very different view of the teachings of Jesus, as the Oxford Group had reconstructed them in the Four Absolutes. These "absolutes" were part of the continuing process of life-change; and, in his last major talk to A.A. at Detroit, Michigan, in 1948, Dr. Bob said:

> The four absolutes, as we called them, were the only yardsticks we had in the early days, before the Steps. I think the absolutes still hold good and can be extremely helpful. I have found at times that a question arises, and I want to do the right thing, but the answer is not obvious. Almost always, if I measure my decision carefully by the yardsticks of absolute honesty, absolute unselfishness, absolute purity, and absolute love, and it checks pretty well with those four, then my answer can't be very far out of the way. If, however, I do that and I'm still not too satisfied with the answer, I usually consult with some friend whose judgment, in this particular case, would be very much better than mine. But usually the absolutes can help you to reach your own personal decision without bothering your friends.[48]

In a personal interview with the author in Akron in June, 1991, Sue Smith Windows said she felt quite sure that her mother and her father endeavored throughout their lives to live by the Four Absolutes. And, as we have shown, Anne Smith mentioned the absolutes often in her Journal. It thus seems that, for the Smiths, it was the *endeavor* to live by the absolutes—spiritual *progress*, rather than spiritual perfection—that counted.

---

[47] (...continued)
often fail of their desired purpose when they are done from our own power alone; that the only real good is accomplished by finding God's plan and then using all of whatever ability He has given us to carry out that plan" (pp. 91-100).

[48] *The Co-Founders of Alcoholics Anonymous*, p. 13.

Restitution

The Oxford Group staunchly believed in making amends or restitution for harms caused.[49] So did Sam Shoemaker.[50] So did the Big Book as reflected by its Ninth Step and by the daily inventory procedure in its Tenth Step.

Anne Smith was no less specific. At page 18, she twice spoke of restitution. Also, on page 26, of "undone restitutions." Discussing barriers to a full surrender on page 43, she asked, "Any restitution I won't make?" On page 44, "Is there an apology I won't make?" Finally, on page 51, she spoke of international restitution. Yet—considering the immense amount of Oxford Group, Shoemaker, and Big Book writing on amends—it is only fair to observe that the quantity of Anne's writing on restitution is not substantial when compared to the other twenty-eight Oxford Group principles she covered in much more detail.

Daily Surrender

This concept is certainly comprehended within the "Continuance" or "Conservation" category of the Five C's. But it deserves separate mention because it is separately labeled in some Oxford Group writing and in Anne's Journal. It bears close resemblance to A.A.'s Step Ten.

The Eight Points of the Oxford Group said:

> The initial surrender to God does not mean that henceforth we shall be asleep to the world around us; that temptations will never assail or sins conquer us again. After surrender we have to work and eat and sleep and laugh and play as before, and in the round

---

[49] See *What Is The Oxford Group?*, pp. 54-64; Russell, *For Sinners Only*, pp. 119-35; Benson, *The Eight Points of the Oxford Group*, pp. 30-43.

[50] See Shoemaker, *The Conversion of the Church*, pp. 47-48; *National Awakening*, p. 5; *The Church Can Save the World*, pp. 120, 127; *God's Control* (New York: Fleming H. Revell, 1939), p. 12.

> of our daily life come situations which cause reactions against our spiritual good resolutions. Sin remains sin. And even if we surrendered to God yesterday, He waits to see if we will surrender the sin of today to Him with as much sincerity as we surrendered our lives yesterday (pp. 45-46).

Anne wrote, "Let your waking thought be surrender, a 100% daily surrender" (p. 18). On page 44, she wrote, "The next step is to make a daily pilgrimage to the Cross with your burden, and to accept forgiveness from God" (p. 44). And on pages 43 and 44, she sets out ten items to review each day, items such as: "Did I fail in loving somebody yesterday?" "Did I compromise anywhere?" "Is there anything I won't give up?"

Quiet Time

Quiet Time was vital to the Oxford Group program. The Group frequently utilized a four-page pamphlet by Howard Rose, titled *The Quiet Time*.[51] The pamphlet contained five parts:

1. *The fact of God's guidance*—occurring through the Holy Spirit in Attentive Prayer, by means of the Scriptures, the Conscience, Luminous Thoughts, and Cultivating the Mind of Christ; through reading the Bible and Prayer; and so on.
2. *The conditions for an effective Quiet Time*—through wholeheartedly giving oneself to Jesus Christ by: (a) willingness to let go every known sin; (b) maintaining right relationships with all men; (c) willingness to make restitution; and (d) adherence to the Four Absolutes; by seeking God, waiting upon God, obedience to the Will of God, and belief in prayer according to the Word.
3. *The tests of God's guidance*—[See "Checking" below].
4. *One method of obtaining God's guidance*—"watch and pray"—relax; confess and seek forgiveness for known sin;

[51] Howard J. Rose, *The Quiet Time* (6 The Green, Slougham, Haywards Heath, Sussex, n.d.).

seek the in-dwelling presence of Christ; dedicate body, soul, and spirit; pray that the Holy Spirit may take charge; have the attitude of "Speak Lord for Thy Servant Heareth;" write down thoughts.

5. *The results of God's guidance*—warnings, actions to take, letters to write, thoughts to share, instructions re prayer, and the like [italics in original].

We have listed the foregoing because, in summary form, they contain almost all the ideas on Guidance and Quiet Time that are discussed at much greater length in a host of leading Oxford Group writings.[52] And Shoemaker wrote frequently about Quiet Time.[53]

The Big Book's Eleventh Step discussion, at pages 85-88, skirts use of the phrase "Quiet Time." However, its references to "meditation," "prayer," asking "God to direct our thinking," asking "God for inspiration, an intuitive thought or a decision," "inspiration," "period of meditation," and "morning meditation," hearken back to the Akron days. For Bill, Dr. Bob, and Anne had daily Quiet Time with Scripture reading and prayer.[54] In later A.A. years, Bill W. was apparently puzzled by the success Akronites Wally and Annabelle G. had in sobering people up in their home. And Wilson made the following observations:

> Maybe they just hit the right cases. There certainly wasn't any difference in the treatment. I think there may have been times

[52] See Cecil Rose, *When Man Listens* (New York: Oxford University Press, 1937); *What Is The Oxford Group?*, pp. 65-72; Jack C. Winslow, *Why I Believe in the Oxford Group* (London: Hodder & Stoughton, 1934), pp. 39-47; *When I Awake* (London: Hodder & Stoughton, 1938); Eleanor Napier Forde, *The Guidance of God* (Oxford: The Oxford Group, 1930); Russell, *For Sinners Only*, pp. 219-36; Streeter, *The God Who Speaks*.

[53] See, for example, Shoemaker, *Realizing Religion*, pp. 65-66; *The Conversion of the Church*, pp. 60-61; *The Church Can Save the World*, p. 126; *Children of the Second Birth*, p. 97.

[54] *DR. BOB*, pp. 71-72, 86, 111, 131, 136. On page 136, Frank Amos pointed out that "Morning devotion and 'quiet time,' however, were musts." See also Kurtz, *Not-God*, pp. 40, 44, 49.

when we attributed it to their morning hour of meditation. . . . I sort of always felt there was something lost from A.A. when we stopped emphasizing the morning meditation (*DR. BOB*, p. 178).

Bill also stated:

> Where did we learn about meditation and prayer and all the rest of it? The spiritual substance of our remaining ten Steps came straight from Dr. Bob's and my own earlier association with the Oxford Groups as they were lead in America by that Episcopal rector, Dr. Samuel Shoemaker.[55]

Anne Smith devoted a good deal of her Journal to discussion of Quiet Time. These are some of her notes:

> *Effective Quiet Time* [italics in original]: (1) Objective: God and obedience. (2) Attentive prayer and being willing to act immediately. (3) Stillness and surrender of all known sins.
> *Results of an effective Quiet time* [italics in original]: (1) Overflowing life. (2) Attitude made clear. (3) Strength for everything. No guidance in the world leaves you out of power and the presence of God (p. 44).

> Quiet Time: . . . What thoughts do I expect? Am I ready to write them down and willing? It is not making my mind a blank but trusting God to use my mind, my thought life and my imagination (p. 18).

> Your attitude in a personal interview should be flexible, antiseptic listening, and unshockable. Have a quiet time (p. 25).

> Write down your guidance, and thus fix your fugitive thought. This is important; it gives you a chance to check guidance with others. When God speaks to you, stop everything to listen. This is the essential of your Quiet Time. Guidance is incidental. It just comes (p. 2).

[55] *The Language of the Heart*, p. 298.

Prayer

What Is The Oxford Group? said:

> Prayer is the natural complement of God Direction. We cannot expect God to talk to us if we do not talk to Him, but to the Oxford Group it is not always essential continually to ask God for help in every move we make, or in every problem of our daily lives. If we have faithfully surrendered our lives to Him, God is our Pilot and knows every movement and thought. When we listen for His guidance during our Quiet Times all requests asked or unasked are answered. . . . Real prayer receives a real answer in any place at any time (p. 69).[56]

Shoemaker wrote in *Realizing Religion*:

> Whatever be one's theories about prayer, two things stand: man will pray as long as God and he exist, and the spiritual life cannot be lived without it. People need to pray, and they pray. But it is an art—the art of discerning God's Will—and one must learn it. For prayer is more than primitive awareness of the supernatural; for us Christians it is the communing of children with Father. Obedience to the Voice which speaks in prayer must ever be the condition of hearing that Voice again (pp. 62-65).[57]

The Big Book says at page 85, "Step Eleven suggests prayer and meditation. We shouldn't be shy on this matter of prayer."

Anne certainly showed her faith in the efficacy of prayer by the amount she wrote, and the degree to which she relied, on prayer. In our discussion of the Eleventh Step, we quoted much on what Anne said about prayer. We add, and in many cases, repeat, these remarks by Anne:

---

[56] See also Walter, *Soul Surgery*, pp. 41-44; Benson, *The Eight Points of the Oxford Group*, 58-69, 79, 153.

[57] See also Shoemaker, *The Conversion of the Church*, p. 60; *National Awakening*, p. 53; *Children of the Second Birth*, pp. 148-49.

> We have ceased to believe in the power of God which can save. We do not sincerely believe in prayer. . . . Is it not written that prayer is inevitably answered? (p. 21).
>
> What do you do when you pray? . . . That we are so in touch with the Holy Spirit that He can give us at that moment a message that is accurate and adequate (p. 26).
>
> Prayer. Why not answered? Until we are ready to fulfill the conditions the deepest wishes of our heart cannot be realized. Intercessory prayer—pray that Spirit may tell you what to pray for. . . . A way to find God's will not to change it. . . . Right orientation of soul towards God. Conceive God as Father and it is not unnatural to lay before Him our hopes and needs--interest--fears. . . . Petitionary prayer—These we submit not because we distrust His goodness or desire to bend His Will but because He is our Friend. . . . If we do not find ourselves desiring to pray for others as we pray for ourselves, we are not traveling in the right direction (p. 58).
>
> Correct me—direct—praise—adoration and thanksgiving—Romans II (p. 59).

Bible Study

Henry Drummond said God gave us two helps in learning how to do His Will: (1) Christ, the Living Word; and (2) the Bible, the written Word. He said that without Christ's Model Life, the ideal life would be incredible, but without the analysis of that life in the Word of God (the Bible), Christ's Model Life would be unintelligible.[58] And Oxford Group people were emphatic as to the importance of studying the Bible.[59] In fact, almost every Oxford Group writing quotes or refers to Bible passages. The reason is

---

[58] Drummond, *The Ideal Life*, p. 231.

[59] See Streeter, *The God Who Speaks* (entire book); Russell, *For Sinners Only*, 94; Benson, *The Eight Points of the Oxford Group*, pp. 58, 78-84.

clear. Dr. Sherwood Day said, "The principles of 'The Oxford Group' are the principles of the Bible."[60]

Dr. Shoemaker repeatedly emphasized the importance of Bible study, stating in *The Conversion of the Church*, for example, "We find God's general will in the Scriptures" (p. 49).[61] Note that, while the Big Book talks much about learning and knowing the Will of God, it does not mention the Bible. Such was not the case in early A.A. For Dr. Bob had said A.A. got its basic ideas from a study of the Bible and that early AA's felt the answer to their problems was in the Bible.[62] And we have already quoted Anne Smith's statement that the Bible should be the principal source book and should be read daily.

Guidance

Because we covered so much of the background in our discussion of Quiet Time, little needs to be said here of Guidance. But Guidance and Quiet Time involve two, separate, distinct ideas.

Quiet Time—though not confined to morning—essentially involved Bible study, prayer, listening, writing down luminous thoughts, and checking. Guidance is perhaps a more general word used to describe God's directing men, nations, and the world where there is obedience to His Will. It was in this arena, that Frank Buchman felt He had been guided to remake the world and bent his efforts and those of Moral Re-Armament to do so.

In *Remaking the World*, Buchman is quoted as follows:

> Leaders everywhere now say that the world needs a moral and spiritual awakening. . . . The problem is how. . . . Now I find when we don't know how, God will show us if we are willing. When man listens, God speaks. When man obeys, God acts. The

---

[60] Day, *The Principles of The Group*. p. 1.

[61] See also Shoemaker, *Realizing Religion*, pp. 58-62; *The Conversion of the Church*, pp. 50, 79; *Children of the Second Birth*, p. 97; *Twice-Born Ministers*, p. 184.

[62] *DR. BOB*, pp. 97, 96, 102, 111, 131.

> secret is God control. We are not out to tell God. We are out to let God tell us. And He will tell us. The lesson the world most needs is the art of listening to God. . . . It is thoughts from God which have inspired the prophets through history (p. 45).
>
> God spoke to the prophets of old. He may speak to you (p. 44).
>
> By a miracle of the Spirit, God can speak to every man (p. 42).
>
> Direct messages from the Mind of God to the mind of man—definite, direct, decisive. God speaks (p. 72).

Shoemaker also confirmed his belief in Guidance. In *With the Holy Spirit and with Fire*, he wrote:

> Another important experience of the Holy Spirit is His guidance. Dr. Van Dusen says, "If there be a Living God at all, He must desire to make His Will and purposes known to men; and a silent, receptive, consciousness furnishes Him the most favorable condition for the disclosure of His thoughts to the minds of men."[63]

There was much talk about, and belief in, Guidance in early A.A.[64] Anne Smith repeatedly spoke of her belief in the Guidance of God (pp. 2, 8-10, 15-16, 27, 31). And the Big Book frequently speaks of asking God for direction (pp. 68-69, 80, 86-87, 100, 164).

---

[63] Samuel M. Shoemaker, *With the Holy Spirit and with Fire* (New York: Harper & Brothers, 1960), pp. 30-31. See also *The Conversion of the Church*, pp. 49-50, 65-66; *National Awakening*, p. 86; *Twice-Born Ministers*, pp. 184-85.

[64] See *DR. BOB*, pp. 57, 86, 115, 313-14; *Pass It On*, pp. 128, 147, 172; *The Language of the Heart*, p. 77; *Lois Remembers*, p. 100; *Alcoholics Anonymous. An Interpretation of Our Twelve Steps* (Washington D.C.: "The Paragon" Creative Printers, no date), pp. 13-14.

Listening for Leading Thoughts and Writing Them Down

Two Bible verses often appeared in Oxford Group-Shoemaker writings as to listening for leading thoughts and writing them down:

1. For the expectant mood of Quiet Time, "Speak LORD; for thy servant heareth" (1 Samuel 3:9).[65]

2. For writing down the ideas and thoughts which the Holy Spirit caused to arise in the mind, "Thus speaketh the LORD God of Israel, saying, 'Write thee all the words that I have spoken unto thee in a book'" (Jeremiah 30:2).[66]

Early AAs wrote down guided thoughts.[67] And Anne had written:

> Write down your guidance, and thus fix your fugitive thoughts. This is important; it gives you a chance to check guidance with others. When God speaks to you, stop everything and listen (p. 2).

Checking

In Bill Wilson's eyes, the Oxford Group practice of "checking" luminous or leading thoughts to make sure they were from God became objectionable.[68] But Frank Buchman had said of "luminous thoughts": "The second rule is that we test the thoughts that come, to see which are from God. One test is the Bible. . . .

---

[65] See, for example, H. Rose, *The Quiet Time*, p. 3; Benson, *The Eight Points of the Oxford Group*, p. 73; Shoemaker, *National Awakening*, pp. 78-88; *God's Control*, p. 115.

[66] See, for example, H. Rose, *The Quiet Time*, p. 3. Compare Buchman, *Remaking the World*, p. 36; *What Is The Oxford Group?*, p. 68; Benson, *The Eight Points of the Oxford Group*, p. 73; C. Rose, *When Man Listens*, p. 37; Shoemaker, *The Conversion of the Church*, pp. 80-81.

[67] *DR. BOB*, p. 86; *Pass It On*, p. 128.

[68] See *Pass It On*, p. 172; *AA Comes of Age*, p. 74.

Another excellent test is, 'What do others say who also listen to God?'"[69] *For Sinners Only* suggested asking about a thought:

> Does it go counter to the highest standards of belief that we already possess? Does it contradict the revelations which Christ has already made in or through the Bible? Is it absolutely honest, pure, unselfish, loving? Does it conflict with our real duties and responsibilities to others? If still uncertain, wait and continue in prayer, and consult a trustworthy friend who believes in the guidance of the Holy Spirit (p. 94).[70]

Shoemaker also wrote on the importance of such "checking."[71]

"Checking" did not make it into the Big Book. But Dr. Bob mentioned it obliquely when he spoke, in his last major address to A.A., about the Four Absolutes as "yardsticks," and consulting a friend when in doubt as to a decision.[72]

In any event, Anne wrote in her Journal a number of times about the practice of "checking." At page 2, she suggested that the listener "check guidance with others." At page 7, she said that checking was "indispensable to creative Christian growth." At page 14, she pointed out that "God's thoughts are not in conflict with the Bible, will stand the test of all four standards," can be tested by circumstances, can be tested with other guided people, and can be tested by action. And at page 31, she mentioned the importance of checking plans with someone else.

---

[69] Buchman, *Remaking the World*, p. 36.

[70] See also H. Rose, *The Quiet Time*, p. 2; C. Rose, *When Man Listens*, pp. 34-35.

[71] See Shoemaker, *The Conversion of the Church*, pp. 51-60; *Twice-Born Ministers*, p. 125.

[72] See *Co-Founders*, p. 13.

Jesus Christ

A reader will find no significant mention of Jesus Christ in today's Big Book text.[73] Dr. Ernest Kurtz made the following observation in *Not-God*:

> The Oxford Group was a conscious attempt to return to primitive fundamental Christianity. The briefest statement of the fundamental Christian message runs: "Jesus saves." The fundamental message of Alcoholics Anonymous, proclaimed by the very presence of a former compulsive drunk standing sober, ran: "Something saves." "Salvation" as the message remained. Yet A.A.'s total omission of "Jesus," its toning down of even "God" to "a Higher Power" which could be the group itself, and its changing of the verbal first message into hopeless helplessness rather than salvation; these ideas and practices, adopted to avoid any "religious" association, were profound changes (p. 50).

The author might agree that Dr. Kurtz's statement is an accurate description of the kind of thinking that pours out of A.A.'s lofty towers in New York in 1998. But one cannot escape the immense influence of Jesus Christ in the sources, language, beliefs, and practices in the trenches of the pioneers in early A.A.

Dr. Bob said that A.A.'s underlying philosophy could be found in Jesus's Sermon on the Mount.[74] He said the Sermon on the Mount and other New Testament Epistles were "absolutely essential" in the early recovery program.[75] He said the Four Absolutes—which were derived from Dr. Robert Speer's reconstruction of the teachings of Jesus Christ—were the *only* "yard-

---

[73] On page 11, Bill did have this to say in his story, "To Christ I conceded the certainty of a great man, not too closely followed by those who claimed Him. His moral teaching—most excellent. For myself, I had adopted those parts which seemed convenient and not too difficult; the rest I disregarded."

[74] *DR. BOB*, p. 228. A.A. historian and author Mel B. personally informed the author that he had heard Bill Wilson say the same thing on more than one occasion.

[75] *DR. BOB*, p. 96.

sticks" early AA's had.[76] He called early A.A. "A Christian Fellowship."[77] And both Frank Amos, reporting on Akron A.A. to John D. Rockefeller, Jr., and Albert Scott, a Rockefeller associate, referred to A.A. as "First Century Christianity."[78]

Thus it is not surprising that Anne's Journal is saturated with references to Jesus Christ (pp. 10, 14-16, 24-25, 36, 41-42, 51). She wrote at page 25 on the "Foundation of this Philosophy" and said, "A maximum experience of Jesus Christ leads to a radical change in personal life, bringing about a selfless relationship to people about one, which is a challenge to those we come in contact with."

As can be seen in other portions of this book, Anne had many things to say about Jesus Christ. She said, "Jesus was in constant touch with the Father" (p. 8). She spoke of our learning through guidance to "think Christ's thoughts" (p. 8). She said "love for Christ" should be the "dominant motive" (p. 10). She said Jesus was "truly the King of Truth" (p. 13). She spoke of "the true way of Jesus Christ" (p. 13). She spoke of "Christ's basic principle, which he expressed in saying that we must love even the very least of them" (p. 19).

As the author was preparing this revision, he received a letter from John F. Seiberling, son of Dr. Bob and Anne's close friend, and early A.A.'s spiritual teacher Henrietta Buckler Seiberling. John sent excerpts from his mother's letters and then said:

> In connection with the quest for the spiritual roots of A.A. and Henrietta's approach in particular: In a nutshell, she was

---

[76] *DR. BOB*, p. 54.

[77] *DR. BOB*, p. 118. This is also confirmed by a handwritten memo from early Akron AA, Bob E., written to Lois Wilson on an Akron "Four Absolutes" pamphlet and which the author inspected and copied during Founders Day at Akron at the 1991 conference there. Sue Smith Windows informed the author in June of 1991 that Dr. Bob called every meeting of the King School Group a "Christian Fellowship."

[78] *DR. BOB*, pp. 129, 136; *Pass It On*. p. 184; compare Robert Thomsen, *Bill W.* (New York: Harper & Row, 1975), p. 282.

determined to stick to St. Paul's resolve "to know nothing but Christ and Him crucified."[79]

The Four Absolutes

We have already been discussing the Four Absolutes—Honesty, Unselfishness, Purity, and Love. We therefore just review here their sources: (1) They can be found in Frank Buchman's speeches.[80] (2) They can be found in books about Buchman.[81] They can be found in descriptions of Oxford Group principles.[82] They can be found in Sam Shoemaker's writings.[83] They are frequently mentioned in A.A.'s conference approved books.[84] They are still prevalent in some A.A. areas today.[85] And many believe that they derived from Dr. Robert E. Speer's reconstruction of the principles of Jesus Christ's Sermon on the Mount.[86] Anne Smith wrote about them frequently in her Journal (pp. 7, 9, 14, 25, 32).

Interestingly, Bill Wilson wound up asserting that the Four Absolutes were included in Steps 6 and 7 of the Big Book. Dr. Ernest Kurtz quotes Bill as follows:

---

[79] See 1 Corinthians 2:1-2: "And I [Paul], brethren, when I came to you, came not with excellency of speech or of wisdom, declaring unto you the testimony of God. For I determined not to know any thing among you, save Jesus Christ, and him crucified."

[80] Buchman, *Remaking the World*, p. 36, 40, 96, 131.

[81] Russell, *For Sinners Only*, pp. 319-329; Lean, *On the Tail of a Comet*, pp. 76-77.

[82] *What Is The Oxford Group?*, pp. 7-8; Benson, *The Eight Points of the Oxford Group*, pp. 44-57; Winslow, *Why I Believe in the Oxford Group*, pp. 24-32.

[83] Shoemaker, *Twice-Born Ministers*, p. 150; *The Church Can Save the World*. p. 119; *How to Become a Christian*, p. 57. See also Helen Smith Shoemaker, *I Stand by the Door* (New York: Harper & Row, 1967), pp. 24-26.

[84] *DR. BOB*, pp. 54, 163; *Pass It On*, pp. 114, 172; *AA Comes of Age*, pp. 68, 161; *The Language of the Heart*, pp. 198-200; *Co-Founders*, pp. 13-14.

[85] Mel B., *New Wine* (Minnesota: Hazelden, 1991), pp. 76, 138.

[86] Shoemaker, *How to Become a Christian*, p. 57; Henry Wright, *The Will of God and a Man's Lifework*, pp. 167-220; Robert E. Speer, *The Principles of Jesus* (New York: Fleming H. Revell, 1902), pp. 33-36; Lean, *On the Tail of a Comet*, p. 76.

> As you so well understand, we drunks are all-or-nothing people. In the old days of the Oxford Groups, they were forever talking about the Four Absolutes—Honesty, Purity, Unselfishness and Love. There we saw people going broke on this sort of perfection—trying to get too good by Thursday. . . . There is another factor, too, which perhaps you have overlooked. Absolutes in themselves are not necessarily destructive. Every sound theological system contains them. When we say that our destiny is to grow in the likeness and image of God, we are stating a healthy relation between a relative and an absolute state of affairs. Therefore when writing the Twelve Steps, it was necessary to include some sort of absolute value or else they wouldn't have been theologically sound. . . . That could have been unfortunate. However, we couldn't make them as promising and as misleading as we found them in the Oxford Group emphasis. So in Steps Six and Seven, and in the use of the word God, we did include them.[87]

Fellowship

In the autumn of 1922, Frank Buchman and a few friends formed what they called "A First Century Christian Fellowship."[88] Harold Begbie's *Life Changers* provided further details about "A First Century Christian Fellowship," saying the fundamental beliefs of First Century Christianity were:

> The possibility of immediate and continued fellowship with the Holy Spirit—guidance.
>
> The proclamation of a redemptive gospel—personal, social, and national salvation.
>
> The possession of the fullness of life—rebirth, and an ever-increasing power and wisdom.

---

[87] Kurtz, *NOT-GOD*, pp. 242-43.

[88] Lean, *On the Tail of a Comet*, p. 97.

> The propagation of their life by individuals to individuals—personal religion (pp. 107-08).

Buchman's "A First Century Christian Fellowship" later became the "Oxford Group," and, in some areas, "Moral Re-Armament." The Group still uses both of the latter names today.

Whatever the name, the Group emphasized *fellowship*.[89] And, as to fellowship, the Oxford Group often cited 1 John 1:3:

> That which we have seen and heard declare we unto you, that ye also may have fellowship with us: and truly our fellowship *is* with the Father, and with His Son Jesus Christ.[90]

Shoemaker often spoke of "fellowship" in terms of the "group," "house-parties," and the fellowship of those who had had a Christian experience.[91] Early Akron AAs called themselves a "Christian Fellowship."[92] And A.A. today calls itself a Fellowship (Big Book, pp. xv, 45, 90). In fact, at page 164, the Big Book says, "We shall be with you in the Fellowship of the Spirit." That language closely resembles the Bible's language concerning the communion or fellowship of the Holy Spirit.

---

[89] *What Is The Oxford Group?*, p. 129; Benson, *The Eight Points of the Oxford Group*, which has an entire chapter entitled, "Lo! Here is the Fellowship" (pp. 102-14).

[90] J. P. Thornton-Duesbury, *Sharing* (Published by The Oxford Group, Printed in Great Britain at the University Press, Oxford by John Johnson, Printer to the University, no date), p. 3; Benson, *The Eight Points of the Oxford Group*, p. 112.

[91] See Shoemaker, *Twice-Born Ministers*, p. 180; *The Conversion of the Church*, pp. 98-101; *With the Holy Spirit and with Fire*, pp. 109-18; *The Gospel According to You*, p. 190; *They're on the Way*, p. 159; and *Religion That Works*—which has a chapter, entitled "The Fellowship of the Holy Ghost" [See 2 Corinthians 13:14]—and speaks of the corporate personality when believers are gathered together and in which the Holy Spirit can communicate His truth to a spiritual fellowship of believers in ways He cannot communicate to individuals. It emphasizes Christ's comment—"where two or three are gathered together in my name" [Matthew 18:20].

[92] *Pass It On*, p. 130. See handwritten memo by Bob E. to Lois Wilson on the Akron A.A. Pamphlet, *Four Absolutes*. As previously stated, Sue Windows informed the author her father called the meetings of the King School Group a "Christian Fellowship."

In any event, Anne echoed a good many Oxford Group comments on Fellowship and quoted 1 John 1:3 (pp. 11, 16, 26, 49-51 of her Journal).

Witness

You have to pass it on! You have to "give it away to keep it." These are everyday A.A. expressions; and they can certainly be found in Oxford Group writings, in Shoemaker writings, and in Anne Smith's Journal. Frank Buchman said, "The best way to keep an experience of Christ is to pass it on."[93] Speaking of the New Testament's offer of a transforming experience of the power and presence of God, Leslie Weatherhead said, "the experience, if truly possessed, is something which others long for when they see it, and is something we want to pass on."[94] Shoemaker often said, "The best way to keep what you have is to give it away."[95]

Anne wrote much on Confidence, service, sharing, saving, helping others, and witness (pp. 2, 5, 11, 13-14, 24-25, 30, 33). But she said things, on page 2 of her Journal, that A.A. later emphasized in Step 12. She said that, first, one must *have* a spiritual experience or spiritual awakening. *Then* he or she is in a position to carry the message. Not the other way around.

As we've mentioned before, Anne wrote:

> A general experience of God is the first essential, the beginning. We can't give away what we haven't got. We must have a genuine contact with God in our present experience. Not an experience of the past, but an experience in the present—actual, genuine. When we have that, witnessing to it is natural, just as we want to share a beautiful sunset. We must be in such close touch with God that

---

[93] Buchman, *Remaking the World*, p. x in the Foreword by Alan Thornhill, quoting Buchman.

[94] Leslie D. Weatherhead, *Discipleship* (New York: The Abingdon Press, 1934), p. 17.

[95] See Shoemaker, *They're on the Way*, p. 159; *How to Become a Christian*, p. 80; *One Boy's Influence* (New York: Association Press, 1923), p. 15.

the whole sharing is guided. The person with a genuine experience of God and with no technique will make fewer mistakes than one with lots of technique and no sense of God. Under guidance, you are almost a spectator of what is happening. Your sharing is not strained, it is not tense. We must clearly see and understand our own experience, and clearly articulate it, so as to be ready to know what to say, or to use parts of it, when the need comes to share with others in order to help them.

Knowing God's Will

The Oxford Group recognized at least two ways in which God makes known His Will.

First, by His Written Word. They said the Bible contained God's General or Universal Will for man—Love, Forgiveness, Salvation, and so on.[96] So a principal reason for study of the Bible is to learn and know the Will of God—God's General or Universal Will, spelled out, for example, in the Sermon on the Mount, 1 Corinthians 13, and the Book of James. And Dr. Bob specified these Bible segments as "absolutely essential" reading.

Second, the Oxford Group strongly believed that God speaks to man via the Holy Spirit. They said that God speaks when man listens and God acts when man obeys.[97] They said God can and does communicate His particular or private will to man through Guidance. That was the reason for Quiet Time, Prayer, Bible study, listening, and checking.[98]

---

[96] See Drummond, *The Ideal Life*, pp. 261-78; and see Shoemaker, *Confident Faith*, (New York: Fleming H. Revell, 1932), pp. 48-49; *The Conversion of the Church*, p. 49; *Christ and This Crisis* (New York: Fleming H. Revell, 1943), p. 106; *The Church Alive* (New York: E.P. Dutton & Co., 1950), pp. 75-76; *The Experiment of Faith* (New York: Harper & Brothers, 1957), pp. 35-36; *How to Become a Christian*, pp. 108-10.

[97] Buchman, *Remaking the World*, pp. 35, 42.

[98] See Shoemaker, *Religion That Works*, pp. 54-64; *The Conversion of the Church*, pp. 47-65; *The Church Can Save the World*, p. 126; *God's Control*, pp. 10-11; *The Gospel According to You* (New York: Fleming H. Revell, 1934), pp. 44-45; *Christ's Words from the Cross* (New York: Fleming H. Revell, 1933), pp. 50-52. See also the (continued...)

Oxford Group people had some significant Bible verses they quoted on God's instructions as to how to receive His Will. One verse—said by *For Sinners Only* to be Shoemaker's favorite verse—is John 7:17:

> If any man will do his will, he shall know of the doctrine, whether it be of God, or *whether* I speak of myself.[99]

The verse appears in dozens of Oxford Group and Shoemaker writings. It is approached in several ways: Drummond said if a man will sincerely try to do God's Will, he will know what God's Will is from the results of his obedient actions. Other writers, such as Brown, in *The Venture of Belief*, indicated that God has a chance to control us and we begin to sense His plan when we honestly seek to know and honestly try to obey the Will of God. The John 7:17 verse is used to emphasize "willingness" as the starting point and "obedience" as the objective. When these are satisfied, God speaks and acts; and man knows His Will.

Another verse that illustrates willingness, and was frequently quoted, is Acts 9:6, "Lord, what wilt thou have me to do?"[100] And then the Lord spoke. Still another has been discussed: "Speak LORD, for Thy servant heareth" [1 Samuel 3:9].[101] Finally, "Be still and know that I am God" [Psalm 46:10].[102]

---

[98] (...continued)
basic Oxford Group books on Guidance: Forde, *The Guidance of God*; C. Rose, *When Man Listens*; Streeter, *The God Who Speaks*; W. E. Sangster, *God Does Guide Us* (New York: The Abingdon Press, 1934).

[99] Drummond, *The Ideal Life*, p. 302; Wright, *The Will of God*, pp. 117, 146; C. Rose, *When Man Listens*, p. 17; Russell, *For Sinners Only*, p. 211; Shoemaker, *Religion That Works*, pp. 46, 58; *A Young Man's View of the Ministry* (New York: Association Press, 1923), p. 41.

[100] Drummond, *The Ideal Life*, p. 306; Shoemaker, *A Young Man's View of the Ministry*, p. 80; *Confident Faith*, p. 107.

[101] C. Rose, *When Man Listens*, p. 30; H. Rose, *The Quiet Time*; Shoemaker, *National Awakening*, pp. 45-54.

[102] Brown, *The Venture of Belief*, p. 37. See also, H. Rose, *The Quiet Time*, p. 1; Shoemaker, *National Awakening*, pp. 45-54.

All these verses emphasize the posture of expectant, willing, waiting for God's directions; a significant and sincere effort to act on what is known, thus signifying obedience; and then confidence that God speaks and acts and makes His Will known when such an approach is taken.

Anne discussed the Bible as the main Source for knowing God's Will; and she also dealt with the concepts of willingness, doing God's Will, and asking what God would have us to do just as Paul did in Acts 9:6 (pp. 6, 8, 16, 42, 61).

God Consciousness

The Oxford Group's sought an "experience of God,"[103] a "vital experience of Jesus Christ,"[104] a "religious experience,"[105] a "spiritual experience,"[106] a spiritual "awakening,"[107] a "relationship with God,"[108] the "power and presence of God,"[109] being "in touch with God,"[110] making "contact" with God,[111]

---

[103] Leon, *The Philosophy of Courage*, p. 110.

[104] Shoemaker, *The Conversion of the Church*, p. 109; *Twice-Born Ministers*, p. 10. Benson, *The Eight Points*, p. xviii—"a maximum experience of Jesus Christ."

[105] Shoemaker, *Realizing Religion*, pp. 4-9. See Big Book, p. 28.

[106] Shoemaker, *Twice-Born Ministers*, p. 10. See Big Book, p. 44.

[107] Shoemaker, *The Conversion of the Church*, p. 124; Buchman, *Remaking the World*, pp. 19, 24, 35, 54. See Big Book, p. 60.

[108] Shoemaker, *Children of the Second Birth*, p. 16; *Christ's Words from the Cross*, p. 50. See Big Book, pp. 28, 29.

[109] Shoemaker, *With the Holy Spirit and with Fire*, pp. 11-12, 15, 27. See Big Book, pp. 51, 56, 63, 162.

[110] Shoemaker, *National Awakening*, pp. 78-88.

[111] Benson, *The Eight Points of the Oxford Group*, p. 31. See the language of the Eleventh Step in the Big Book, p. 59.

a "conversion,"[112] a "surrender,"[113] "change,"[114] being "born again,"[115] and "God consciousness."[116]

Anne used the following similar expressions in her Journal: experience of God (pp. 2, 12, 20); relationship with God (pp. 8, 37, 42, 62); in touch with God (p. 30); contact with God (p. 2); conversion (pp. 4, 28); surrender (pp. 13, 16-17, 26, 42, 45, 56, 61); change (pp. 4, 23, 27, 57); the new birth (pp. 6, 42); God-consciousness (pp. 13, 19).

For the same or similar language in the Big Book, see: (1) a relationship with God, pp. 13, 28, 29, 72, 100, 164, 452; (2) contact with God, pp. 46, 47, 56, 59, 63, 87; (3) surrender, pp. 271, 272; (4) change, xxvii, 50, 51, 84, 569, 572; (5) rebirth, p. 63; and (6) God-consciousness, pp. 13, 85, 569, 570.

---

[112] Shoemaker, *Realizing Religion*, pp. 22-35. See *Pass It On*, pp. 381-86.

[113] *What Is The Oxford Group?*, p. 43; Shoemaker, *Children of the Second Birth*, p. 16. See *DR. BOB*, pp. 77, 89, 92-93, 110, 139, 141.

[114] Mel B., *New Wine*, p. 23; Dennis C. Morreim, *Changed Lives* (Minneapolis: Augsburg, 1991), p. 24. See Big Book, pp. 569-70.

[115] Samuel M. Shoemaker, *Twice-Born Ministers*, pp. 10, 56; *By the Power of God* (New York: Harper & Brothers, 1954), pp. 28-33, 105; *They're on the Way*, p. 157. Buchman, *Remaking the World*, p. 23; See Big Book, p. 63. In an early draft of the Big Book which the author inspected at Bill's home at Stepping Stones, Bill used the expression "born again" to describe his "white flash" spiritual experience at Towns Hospital. His "born again" language has disappeared from official A.A. publications.

[116] Begbie, *Life Changers*, pp. 16, 39. Leon, *The Philosophy of Courage*, p. 110-11. See Big Book, pp. 13, 85, 569-70.

5

Spiritual Principles

Oxford Group Principles

About 1926, Dr. Samuel M. Shoemaker encouraged the Reverend Sherwood S. Day to outline the primary New Testament principles which he and Day had learned to accept together and which had come to form a central part of Dr. Shoemaker's own credo. In one of the 1926 issues of *The Calvary Evangel*—the parish publication of Dr. Shoemaker's Calvary Church in New York—Reverend Day summed up those convictions.[1] Day's summary was also published by The Oxford Group in an eleven-page pamphlet titled *The Principles of the Oxford Group*.[2] A. J. Russell expanded upon these principles in *For Sinners Only*.[3]

In *The Principles of the Oxford Group* pamphlet, the Rev. Day commenced with the statement, "The principles of 'The Oxford Group' are the principles of the Bible" (p. 3).

---

[1] Irving Harris, *The Breeze of the Spirit: Sam Shoemaker and the Story of Faith at Work* (New York: The Seabury Press, 1978), pp. 18-21.

[2] Sherwood Sunderland Day, *The Principles of the Oxford Group* (pamphlet published by The Oxford Group and printed in Great Britain at the University Press, Oxford, by John Johnson, Printer to the University, no date).

[3] A. J. Russell, *For Sinners Only* (London: Hodder and Stoughton, Ltd., 1932), pp. 23, 27, 42-43.

It is not our intention here to discuss Sherry Day's seven principles at any length; for they are reviewed in detail in our title, *New Light on Alcoholism.*[4] Most of Anne's treatment of these principles can be found in Chapter Two of our present book. However, from our observation of Anne's language, we believe she had these very principles before her in some form as she was writing; for she dealt with each specifically. We therefore list Day's principles and document in our footnotes the places were Anne's specific discussion of them can be found.

Day said, "It is never possible to find Life—peace with God—victory—power by merely trying to follow out principle." He said, "That life comes to one as a possession through but one gateway—a personal experience of Jesus Christ and Him crucified."[5] Day said further that the Oxford Group was a life—that life which is hid in Christ with God; and that the following principles are revelations or pictures of what is bound to take place in any life that is surrendered to the Will of God:

1. ***God-guidance.*** Day said "guidance" meant "communion with our Father, the Living God . . . listening to God . . . two-way prayer . . . thinking God's thoughts after Him."[6]

2. ***Fearless dealing with sin.*** Day said, "The first great fact of history is Jesus Christ, the second is the presence of sin." He said the Bible frankly faces the fact of sin and offers a cure. He said Jesus Christ faced men honestly and fearlessly, gave them courage to do the same with themselves, and then showed them the way out.[7]

---

[4] See Dick B., *New Light on Alcoholism: The A.A. Legacy from Sam Shoemaker* (CA: Good Book Publishing Company, 1994), pp. 68-72.

[5] Day, *The Principles of the Group*, pp. 3-4.

[6] Anne discussed "God-guidance" and "two-way prayer" at pages 2, 8, 9, 10, 15, 16, 27, 31, 38, 47, 50, 51, 58, 59.

[7] Anne discussed these points at pages 4, 13, 16, 34, 38, 48. And it is interesting that the Big Book's Fourth Step self examination language stated, "Made a searching and fearless moral inventory of ourselves."

3. ***Sharing.*** Day said, "A sharing Christian is a propagating Christian" (p. 6). He said, "sharing," as used by the Group, covered two distinct things, further described as confession and witness. Quoting James 5:16, Day said it was necessary to "confess your faults one to another" (p. 6). Anne covered the same point (pp. 32, 33, 4, 5, 25, 34). Day then said sharing, or witnessing, was necessary in helping others. It established confidence because the person confessed to know that the confessor had been through a like experience. Anne made these same points (pp. 2-3, 5, 11, 13, 25, 33, 46, 51, 55).

4. ***The necessity for adequate, intelligent, expressional activity.*** Day urged "a God-guided, released life with constant outgo into the lives of needy people." Anne also stressed, as Day put it, "using one's spiritual muscles to maintain spiritual health" (pp. 13-14, 25, 33, 46, 51, 55).

5. ***Stewardship.*** Day pointed out "that He who bought us with a price owns us and all that He has entrusted to us. On such a basis houses, lands, money, things, relationships, gifts, all that we are and have, make up a trust which we are to administer" (p. 8). Anne also emphasized such stewardship (pp. 16, 31, 39-40).

6. ***Team-work.*** Day said Jesus Christ believed in team-work. He gathered a small group about him and set the example for all his followers in this respect. The Oxford Group often characterized its volunteer-activist groups as "teams." And Anne spoke much about "teams" and teamwork (pp. 12, 15, 26).

7. ***Loyalty.*** Day said, "The supreme loyalty in life should be to Jesus Christ, but . . . the person or group of persons embodying for us the highest challenge we know, the person or persons that have been used to reveal Jesus Christ to us,

are persons and groups which demand our loyalty." And Anne also espoused this loyalty (pp. 12, 15, 25).

Biblical Principles

As previously stated, Reverend Day said the principles of the Oxford Group were the principles of the Bible; and Anne's sixty-four page Journal is liberally salted with Biblical principles and references. She emphasized the following:

1. John 15:13-17.[8] Anne said these verses represent the "maximum perspective of our task as Christians" (p. 2).

2. John 4—"Jesus talk with the Samaritan woman at the well"—for the Oxford Group "Confidence" concept and "How to interview" (p. 5).

3. The Epistle of 1 John for the concept that we love God because He first loved us and sent His Son for the propitiation of our sins (p. 6).[9]

4. 1 John 1:3 for the concept of fellowship with believers and the Heavenly Father (pp. 11, 16).[10]

---

[8] Jesus said: "Greater love hath no man than this, that a man lay down his life for his friends. Ye are my friends, if ye do whatsoever I command you. Henceforth I call you not servants; for the servant knoweth not what his lord doeth: but I have called you friends; for all things that I have heard of my Father I have made known unto you. Ye have not chosen me, but I have chosen you, and ordained you, that ye should go and bring forth fruit, and *that* your fruit should remain: that whatsoever ye shall ask of the Father in my name, he may give it you. These things I command you, the ye love one another."

[9] 1 John 4:10, "Herein is love, not that we loved God, but that he loved us, and sent his Son *to be* the propitiation for our sins."

[10] 1 John 1:3, "That which we have seen and heard declare we unto you, that ye also may have fellowship with us: and truly our fellowship *is* with the Father, and with his Son Jesus Christ."

5. The Epistle of 3 John for God's Will that all should "prosper and be in health" (p. 12).[11]

6. 1 Corinthians 13 for the concept of Love (p. 15). Both Anne and Dr. Bob read Kagawa's *Love: The Law of Life*, and Anne devoted three full pages to a discussion of Kagawa's book (pp. 19-21).[12]

7. Ephesians 4:8-11 for the proposition that divinely endowed leaders have been taken out of captivity to sin, brought into captivity for Christ, and given as a gift to men by the ascended Christ (p. 23).[13]

8. James 5:16 for confession (p. 32).[14]

9. Ephesians 4:15 for speaking the truth in love (p. 33).[15]

10. Sharing as a concept direct from the Gospel—citing Matthew 3:6; Mark 1:5; Matthew 4:1-11; James 5:16; Acts 26:22; 2 Corinthians 5:21 (p. 34). These verses all are foundational for Oxford Group practices of Sharing for Confession and Sharing for Witness.[16]

---

[11] 3 John 2, "Beloved, I wish above all things that thou mayest prosper and be in health, even as thy soul prospereth."

[12] Toyohiko Kagawa, *Love: The Law of Life* (Philadelphia: The John C. Winston Company, 1929).

[13] Ephesians 4:8, 11, "Wherefore he saith, When he ascended up on high, he led captivity captive, and gave gifts unto men . . . And he gave some, apostles; and some, prophets; and some, evangelists; and some, pastors and teachers."

[14] James 5:16, "Confess *your* faults one to another, and pray for one another, that ye may be healed. The effectual fervent prayer of a righteous man availeth much."

[15] Ephesians 4:15, "But speaking the truth in love, may grow up into him in all things, which is the head, *even* Christ."

[16] Matthew 3:6, "And were baptized of him in Jordan, confessing their sins;" Mark 1:5, "And there went out unto him all the land of Judaea, and they of Jerusalem, and were all baptized of him in the river of Jordan, confessing their sins;" Matthew 4:1-11,

(continued...)

11. Romans 12 for the transformation and regeneration that occurs through the power of Christ (p. 36).[17]

12. Romans 8 for the power of the Holy Spirit that brings about change (p. 39).[18]

13. Matthew 6:33 for seeking the Kingdom of God first (p. 39).[19]

14. Acts 5 for the truth of Gamaliel's warning that if teachings about Jesus Christ are of God, they cannot be overthrown (p. 41).[20]

15. Rebirth, reunion with Christ, revival which she said involve decision, discipline and dare—the doing of

---

[16] (...continued)
"Then was Jesus led up of the Spirit into the wilderness to be tempted of the devil . . . But he answered and said, It is written, Man shall not live by bread alone, but by every word that proceedeth out of the mouth of God. . . . Jesus said unto him, It is written again, Thou shalt not tempt the Lord thy God. . . . it is written, Thou shalt worship the Lord thy God, and him only shalt thou serve . . .;" James 5:16 (confess your faults); Acts 26:22 . . . "Having therefore obtained help of God, I continue unto this day, witnessing both to small and great . . .;" 2 Corinthians 5:20-21, "Now then we are ambassadors for Christ . . ."

[17] Romans 12:1-2, "I beseech you therefore, brethren, by the mercies of God, that ye present your bodies a living sacrifice, holy, acceptable unto God, *which is* your reasonable service. And be not conformed to this world: but be ye transformed by the renewing of your mind, that ye may prove what *is* that good, and acceptable, and perfect, will of God."

[18] Romans 8:11, "But if the Spirit of him that raised up Jesus from the dead dwell in you, he that raised up Christ from the dead shall also quicken your mortal bodies by his Spirit that dwelleth in you."

[19] Matthew 6:33, "But seek ye first the kingdom of God, and his righteousness; and all these things shall be added unto you."

[20] Acts 5:38-39, "And now I say unto you, Refrain from these men, and let them alone: for if this counsel or this work be of men, it will come to nought; But if it be of God, ye cannot overthrow it; lest haply ye be found even to fight against God."

definite things—citing, in other parts of the Journal, verses in Matthew, Romans, and James (p. 42).

16. Romans 12:11 and Galatians 1:23 for "maintaining the spiritual glow" by continuing to serve God—"fervent in the spirit"—after surrender has been accomplished (p. 46).[21]

17. The Beatitudes in the Sermon on the Mount for the Christ-like virtues to be cultivated (p. 60).[22]

18. 1 Samuel 15:22: There is a sense of being saved only when preceded by moral destitution, being lost, bankrupt; and then God is not interested in sacrifices, but in obedience and listening (p. 63).[23]

Miscellaneous

Anne mentioned some other points that will sound familiar to AAs. For example, she discussed the *Group* (pp. 3, 26, 52-53);[24] trust in God (p. 9);[25] the forgiveness of God (p. 13);[26] being of

---

[21] Romans 12:11, "Not slothful in business; fervent in spirit; serving the Lord." Galatians 1:23, "But they had heard only, That he [the Apostle Paul] which persecuted us in times past now preacheth the faith which once he destroyed."

[22] Matthew 5:3-11, "Blessed are 'the poor in spirit' . . . 'they that mourn' . . . 'the meek' . . . 'they which do hunger and thirst after righteousness' . . . 'the merciful' . . . 'the pure in heart' . . . 'the peacemakers' . . . 'they which are persecuted for righteousness sake' . . . 'ye, when men shall revile you, and persecute you, and shall say all manner of evil against you falsely, for my sake.'"

[23] 1 Samuel 15:22, "And Samuel said, Hath the Lord *as great* delight in burnt offerings and sacrifices, as in obeying the voice of the Lord? Behold, to obey *is* better than sacrifice, *and* to hearken than the fat of rams."

[24] See Big Book, p. 564, in which A.A. Traditions Two, Four, Five, Six, and Seven deal with the A.A. *group*.

[25] See Big Book, pp. 68 and 98 for "trust in God."

[26] See Big Book, p. 86, "we ask God's forgiveness."

"maximum service to God" (p. 15);[27] patience, tolerance, humility, and love (pp. 6, 17-18, 37, 43);[28] courage, faith, peace, power, and joy (pp. 17, 24).[29] Yes—and a "day at a time!" Anne suggested, at page 9, "Be willing to live a day at a time, an hour at a time." Dr. Bob once commented that the A.A. motto "Easy does it" meant you take it a day at a time.[30] Also, that the expression came from Matthew 6:25 and 6:34 in Jesus's Sermon on the Mount.[31]

---

[27] See Big Book, p. 77, "to be of maximum service to God . . ."

[28] Compare Big Book, p. 83: "patience, tolerance, kindliness and love." And see, as to humility, pp. 13, 73, 57, 63, 68.

[29] Compare Big Book, page 68, "All men of faith have courage;" page 63 as to peace of mind and Power; page 133, "happy, joyous, and free."

[30] *DR. BOB*, p. 282.

[31] See Dick B., *That Amazing Grace: The Role of Clarence and Grace S. in Alcoholics Anonymous* (San Rafael, CA: Paradise Research Publications, 1996), p. 38.

6

Conclusion

History has played out a strange hand as far as recognition of the roles and the anonymity of A.A.'s founders is concerned.

A newcomer to Alcoholics Anonymous is not long in the A.A. Fellowship without learning that if he asks a stranger, "Are you a friend of Bill W.," he can quickly discover from the answer whether he is speaking to someone involved in A.A.'s Fellowship. The newcomer may soon see, on the literature table of an A.A. meeting, its "Conference Approved" book, *As Bill Sees It*. Or, on opening A.A.'s basic textbook, *Alcoholics Anonymous*, may encounter "Bill's Story" on page one. Or, on attending a large conference, may see the A.A. video, "Bill's Story," which features Bill Wilson recounting the A.A. story and chatting with his wife, Lois, about it. And, though not a "member" of Al-Anon, the author soon learned that *Lois Remembers* is an important Al-Anon "Conference Approved" book written by Bill's wife, Lois. And, sooner or later in A.A., one will see *The Language of the Heart*, which contains all the articles Bill Wilson wrote for A.A.'s official, monthly journal, the *AA Grapevine*.

Strange, however, is the totally different picture involving the lives of Dr. Bob and Anne Smith. Bill Wilson did generously dub Dr. Bob "Prince of Twelfth Steppers;" and he characterized Anne Ripley Smith as the "Mother of A.A." Yet few AAs today know either those names or those titles. Nor are they familiar with much of anything about Dr. Bob and Anne. Dr. Bob's "story" is still included in the personal narrative portion of A.A.'s Big Book, but it is not a part of the "basic text" in the first 164 pages. There are no "Conference Approved" videos containing the details about A.A.'s founding in Akron (though a private foundation there has published a video about some of the Akron A.A. story). And A.A. provides little about what Dr. Bob really taught since Dr. Bob did very little writing for A.A.; and very few of his talks to AAs were taped. There is no "Anne Remembers;" and there is only one significant "Conference Approved" book about either of the Smiths. It is *DR. BOB and the Good Oldtimers*.

Dr. Bob and Anne themselves would probably be the first to applaud this state of affairs. For theirs was not a mission of publicity-seeking or self-aggrandizement. They seemed totally focused on love and service. And that, no doubt, is how they would prefer to be remembered.

Nonetheless, we found our journey along the road of Bob and Anne Smith history to be exciting, rewarding, and highly useful. We took seriously the Big Book's suggestion that there were many helpful "outside" books AAs should use for spiritual growth. We took seriously Bill Wilson's repeated comment that A.A. is just a "spiritual kindergarten," and hence his implication that material other than that in A.A. is needed for spiritual growth. We took seriously Dr. Bob's declaration that A.A. got its basic ideas from the Bible; and Bill Wilson's assertion that the spiritual principles came from the Oxford Group, and particularly from one of their American leaders, Reverend Sam Shoemaker. And we found that Anne Smith's Journal held the critical key to information about all these areas of spiritual history and spiritual growth. Areas that assured A.A. the seventy-five percent success rate it had in the early years.[1]

---

[1] See Big Book, p. xx; *A Program for You: A Guide to the Big Book's Design for Living* (MN: Hazelden, 1991), p. 15; Dick B., *Dr. Bob's Library: Books for Twelve Step Growth* (San Rafael, CA: Paradise Research Publications, 1994), pp. 101-02.

Much of the insight to be gained from Anne's Journal has all but vanished from the A.A. Fellowship and its literature. The author has been blessed in his own recovery to discover the importance and relevance of Anne's Journal to the early, high success rate in Akron A.A. Dr. Bob's reading list included more than one hundred titles, and probably inspired the reading of hundreds, and perhaps thousands of early AAs. Yet Dr. Bob's Library is virtually unknown today, though we have personally seen a great hunger in A.A. for this very inspirational source material. More so each day, as A.A.'s spiritual roots are becoming known.

Anne Smith's spiritual journal has gathered dust in New York and in Akron for years. It is a spiritual resource almost unheard of in A.A. Yet, if one wants a good look at the ideas Bill Wilson and the early AAs were studying and hearing during A.A.'s formative years, there is no better source. If one wants to know what was said about the Bible, Christianity, and religion in early A.A., Anne's Journal is a rich resource. If one wants to know what AAs were really learning from the Bible, their daily devotionals, their religious reading, the Oxford Group, and Reverend Sam Shoemaker, the pages of Anne's Journal provide very informative answers. If one wants to see a large amount of the language Bill Wilson later incorporated in the Twelve Steps and A.A. literature, Anne Smith's Journal represents an authoritative, early source. And if one wishes to learn what the "Mother of A.A." was sharing with and teaching early AAs and their families, when the A.A. success rate was phenomenal, her Journal is the place to look.

Bill Wilson, and many other early AAs, long ago heaped accolades on Anne Smith for her love, sacrifice, and service. Praise that was well-deserved and hardly overstated. Bill showed his respect for Anne's contribution to A.A. by asking her to write a chapter of the Big Book. But we did not write this book simply to praise Anne or her contributions to A.A., Al-Anon, and Twelve Step principles and practices. Rather, we hope all who love the A.A. Fellowship and the inspiration and sacrifices of its founders will use this book as a starting point for their own journey. A journey toward the kind of love and service that has made A.A. the indispensable life-line to recovery from alcoholism that it was for the author himself. It is not *who* Anne Smith was that has made a difference in history. It is *what* she wrote, and said, and did. And we hope this book tells a substantial part of the story.

AAs often say that theirs is a program of action. And some, who know A.A.'s early history, are familiar with the popularity of the Book of James as an early recovery tool. James was, in fact, a particular favorite with Dr. Bob and Anne. And both epitomized the proper response to the call in James 1:22-25:

> But be ye doers of the word [the Word of God, Dr. Bob's *Good Book*], and not hearers only, deceiving your own selves. For if any be a hearer of the word, and not a doer, he is like unto a man beholding his natural face in a glass: For he beholdeth himself, and goeth his way, and straightway forgetteth what manner of man he was. But whoso looketh into the perfect law of liberty, and continueth *therein*, he being not a forgetful hearer, but a doer of the work, this man shall be blessed in his deed.

Anne took to heart the lessons she learned from her daily Bible study, prayer, and meditation. She applied them in her home, in group quiet times, and with people she personally helped at meetings and on the telephone. She was a "doer" of the word. She walked the walk she talked. She exemplified for all of us the truth of the A.A. legacy: "You have to give it away to keep it." For she did!

END

Appendix

Twenty-eight Oxford Group Principles That Influenced A.A.

See Chapter Four for Anne's discussion of the twenty-eight Oxford Group principles. Here, our footnotes identify the places in the Bible, in Oxford Group books, in Shoemaker's writings, and in A.A. literature where the ideas can be found:

The Twenty-eight Oxford Group Ideas

In the beginning, God.

1. *God*—Biblical descriptions of Him as Creator, Maker, Father, Spirit, Love, Living God.[1]

---

[1] In this, and in each succeeding, footnote, we identify the four categories where the Oxford Group ideas can be found: a) **Bible**: "Creator" (Isaiah 40:28); "Maker" (Psalm 95:6); "Father" (Matthew 5:45); "Spirit" (John 4:24); "Love" (1 John 4:8); "Living God" (Acts 14:15). b) Oxford Group writings (henceforth, "**Oxford Group**"): Philip M. Brown, *The Venture of Belief* (New York: Fleming H. Revell, 1935), pp. 24-25; Geoffrey Allen, *He That Cometh* (New York: The Macmillan Company, 1933), pp. 222-23; Clarence I Benson, *The Eight Points of the Oxford Group* (Oxford: Oxford University Press, 1936), p. 73; Frank Buchman, *Remaking the World* (London: Blandford Press, 1961), p. 13. c) **Shoemaker**: *The Conversion of the Church* (New York: Fleming H. Revell, 1932), pp. 33, 49, 50, 51, 124; *National Awakening* (New York: Harper & Brothers, 1936), pp. 48, 55, 97, 107, 108; *Confident Faith* (New York: Fleming H. Revell, 1932), pp. 38, 54, 59, 74, 83, 96, 106, 107, 152, 183; *Realizing Religion* (New York: Association Press, 1921), p. 35; *Children of the Second Birth* (New York: Fleming H. Revell, 1927), p. 42; *Christ's Words from the Cross* (New York: Fleming H. Revell, 1933), p. 43. d) In A.A. (henceforth, "**A.A.**"), see in the Big Book: Creator (p. 13), Maker (p. 57), Father (p. 62), Spirit (p. 84); Living God (An early draft of the Big Book contained this phrase, which was later modified to "God" at page 29). See also *DR. BOB and the Good Oldtimers* (New York: Alcoholics Anonymous World Services, 1980), pp. 117, 110; *Pass It On* (New York: Alcoholics Anonymous World Services, 1984), p. 121.

2. *God has a plan*—His will for man—and provides definite, accurate information for the individual who wants the plan fulfilled.[2]

3. *Man's chief end*—To do God's Will, thereby receiving the blessings God promises to those who align their lives with His Will.[3]

4. *Belief*—We must start with the belief that God IS.[4]

Sin—Estrangement from God—The Barrier of Self.

5. *Sin is a reality*—The selfishness and self-centeredness that blocks man from God and from others.[5]

---

[2] a) **Bible**: Jeremiah 7:23; Isaiah 14:5; Proverbs 3:5-6. b) **Oxford Group**: Buchman, *Remaking the World*, pp. 8, 48; Horace Bushnell, *The New Life* (London: Strahan & Co., 1868), pp. iii, 1; Henry B. Wright, *The Will of God* (New York: Y.M.C.A. Press, 1909), p. 3; Brown, *The Venture of Belief*, p. 40. c) **Shoemaker**: *Children of the Second Birth*, p. 27; *Religion That Works* (N.Y.: Fleming H. Revell, 1928), p. 19; *National Awakening*, pp. 41, 83, 89-98. d) **A.A.**: *DR. BOB*, p. 45; cf. *Lois Remembers* (N.Y.: Al-Anon Family Group Headquarters, 1987), p. 100; Big Book, pp. 208-09; 302-03.

[3] a) **Bible**: Acts 13:22; Matthew 6:32-33. b) **Oxford Group**: Henry Drummond, *The Ideal Life* (N.Y.: Hodder & Stoughton, 1897), pp. 227-43; Wright, *The Will of God*, p. 9; Benson, *The Eight Points*, pp. 12-13; B. H. Streeter, *The God Who Speaks* (London: Macmillan, 1943), p. 11. c) **Shoemaker**: *National Awakening*, pp. 42, 47; *Christ's Words from the Cross*, p. 50. d) **A.A.**: Big Book, Step Eleven, and pp. 164, 77.

[4] a) **Bible**: Hebrews 11:6. b) **Oxford Group**: Brown, *The Venture of Belief*, p. 24; Philip Leon, *The Philosophy of Courage* (N.Y.: Oxford University Press, 1939), p. 19; The Layman with a Notebook, *What Is The Oxford Group?* (N.Y.: Oxford University Press, 1933), Foreword. c) **Shoemaker**: *National Awakening*, pp. 40-41; *Children of the Second Birth*, p. 40; *Religion That Works*, p. 55; *Confident Faith*, p. 187. d) **A.A.**: Big Book, p. 53—a virtual quote of Shoemaker's *Confident Faith* language.

[5] a) **Bible**: Romans 3:23. b) **Oxford Group**: A. J. Russell, *For Sinners Only* (London: Hodder & Stoughton, 1932), p. 61. c) **Shoemaker**: *They're on the Way* (New York: E.P Dutton & Co., 1951), p. 154. d) **A.A.**: *Pass It On*, p. 197; Big Book, pp. 60-64, 66, 71, 76.

Finding or Rediscovering God.

6. *Surrender*—The turning point which makes it possible for man to have a relationship with God by surrendering his will, ego, and sins to God.[6]

7. *Soul-Surgery*—The "art" or way which enables man through the steps of Confidence, Confession, Conviction, Conversion, and Conservation (the Five C's) to have the sin or spiritual disease cured.[7]

8. *Life-change*—The result in which man, through a spiritual experience, becomes God-centered instead of self-centered and focuses on helping others.[8]

The Path They Followed to Establish a Relationship with God.

9. *Decision*—The action by which man verbalizes his surrender and gives in to God, saying, essentially, "Thy will be done."[9]

10. *Self-examination*—A "moral" inventory in which man takes stock of his sins and their consequences.[10]

---

[6] a) **Bible**: Acts 3:19. b) **Oxford Group**: Benson, *The Eight Points*, p. 5. c) **Shoemaker**: *The Church Can Save the World* (New York: Harper & Brothers, 1938), pp. 113-14. d) **A.A.**: Big Book, p. 59.

[7] b) **Oxford Group**: Howard A. Walter, *Soul Surgery: Some Thoughts on Incisive Personal Work* (Calcutta, India: Association Press, 1919). c) **Shoemaker**: *The Conversion of the Church*, p. 12; *Realizing Religion*, pp. 79-80. d) **A.A.**: *DR. BOB*, p. 54; Ernest Kurtz, *Not-God: A History of Alcoholics Anonymous*, exp. ed. (MN: Hazelden, 1991), pp. 48-49, 228; Richmond Walker, *For Drunks Only: One Man's Reaction to Alcoholics Anonymous* (1945; reprint, MN: Hazelden, n.d.), pp. 45-46.

[8] a) **Bible**: John 3:3. b) **Oxford Group**: Harold Begbie, *Life Changers* (New York: G. P. Putnam, 1927). c) **Shoemaker**: *The Church Can Save the World*, p. 153. d) **A.A.**: Big Book, pp. 63, 569-70.

[9] a) **Bible**: Matthew 6:10. b) **Oxford Group**: *What Is The Oxford Group?*, pp. 46-48. c) **Shoemaker**: *Children of the Second Birth*, pp. 58, 175-87. d) **A.A.**: Big Book, pp. 60, 63.

[10] a) **Bible**: Matthew 7:3-5. b) **Oxford Group**: Buchman, *Remaking the World*, pp. 3, 24, 28, 38, 46; Walter, *Soul Surgery*, pp. 41-48, 69; Benson, *The Eight Points*, pp. 44, 162, 18, 7; Cecil Rose, *When Man Listens* (New York: Oxford University Press, 1937), pp. 17-19. c) **Shoemaker**: *The Conversion of the Church*, pp. 30-34; *Twice-Born Ministers* (New York: Fleming H. Revell, 1929), p. 182; *How to Become a Christian* (New York: Harper & Brothers, 1953), pp. 56-67; *God's Control* (New York: Fleming H. Revell, 1939), pp. 104-05. d) **A.A.**: Big Book, pp. xvi; *Alcoholics Anonymous Comes of Age* (New York: Alcoholics Anonymous World Services, 1957), p. 39.

11. *Confession*—Sharing with God and another person the inventory results.[11]

12. *Conviction*—Readiness to change resulting from man's conviction that he has sinned and that Christ miraculously can cure.[12]

13. *Conversion*—The New Birth, Change, namely, that which occurs when man gives himself to God, is regenerated, has part of God's nature imparted to him, and finds the barrier of sin gone.[13]

14. *Restitution*—Righting the wrongs and enabling man to cut the cord of sin that binds him to the past.[14]

Jesus Christ

15. *Jesus Christ*—The source of power as the Divine Redeemer and Way-Shower by whose transforming power man can be changed.[15]

---

[11] a) **Bible**: James 5:16. b) **Oxford Group**: J. P. Thornton-Duesbury, *Sharing* (Pamphlet of the Oxford Group, published at Oxford University, n.d.), p. 5; Benson, *The Eight Points*, p. 18. c) **Shoemaker**: *The Conversion of the Church*, p. 35. d) **A.A.**: *Pass It On*, p. 128; Big Book, Step 5.

[12] a) **Bible**: Psalm 65:3. b) **Oxford Group**: Walter, *Soul Surgery*, pp. 64-78. c) **Shoemaker**: *Realizing Religion*, p. 81. d) **A.A.**: See Mel B., *New Wine: The Spiritual Roots of the Twelve Step Miracle* (MN: Hazelden, 1991), pp. 34-35; Big Book, Step 6.

[13] a) **Bible**: John 3:3-4. b) **Oxford Group**: Allen, *He That Cometh*, pp. 19-43. c) **Shoemaker**: *National Awakening*, pp. 55, 57-58. d) **A.A.**: Big Book, pp. 63, 76; *Pass It On*, pp. 381-86.

[14] a) **Bible**: Numbers 5:6-7; Matthew 5:23-24. b) **Oxford Group**: Russell, *For Sinners Only*, p. 119. c) **Shoemaker**: *The Conversion of the Church*, pp. 47-48. d) **A.A.**: Big Book, Steps 8 and 9.

[15] a) **Bible**: John 14:6. b) **Oxford Group**: Brown, *The Venture of Belief*, p. 49. c) **Shoemaker**: *With the Holy Spirit and with Fire* (New York: Harper & Brothers, 1960), pp. 29-33. d) **A.A.**: Compare Kurtz, *Not-God*, p. 50; Dick B., *The Oxford Group & Alcoholics Anonymous* (WA: Glen Abbey, 1992), pp. 197-98; *Dr. Bob's Library* (WV: The Bishop of Books, 1992), pp. ix, 12, 37, 39-42; and *DR. BOB*, pp. 53-54, 141, 148, 163, 183.

Spiritual Growth—Continuance.

16. *Conservation*—Continuance as an idea, by which man maintains and grows in his life of grace.[16]

17. *Daily Surrender*—A process in which man engages in daily self-examination and surrender to get rid of newly accumulated sin and selfishness.[17]

18. *Guidance*—The walk by faith in which the Holy Spirit gives Divine Guidance to a life that is changed from sin to God.[18]

19. *The Four Absolutes*—Christ's standards, the standards of absolute honesty, purity, unselfishness, and love, by which man's life can be tested for harmony with God's will.[19]

20. *Quiet Time*—A period in which man can receive Divine Guidance and be sensitive to the sway of the Spirit.[20]

---

[16] a) **Bible**: Galatians 2:20; Romans 12:1-2. b) **Oxford Group**: Walter, *Soul Surgery*, pp. 89-100; Howard J. Rose, *The Quiet Time* (NY: The Oxford Group, 61 Gramercy Park North, n.d.), p. 2. c) **Shoemaker**: *Realizing Religion*, p. 80; *Religion That Works*, pp. 14-15. d) **A.A.**: Big Book, pp. 83-85.

[17] a) **Bible**: Matthew 26:41; John 16:13-16. b) **Oxford Group**: Benson, *The Eight Points*, pp. 45-46; H. Rose, *The Quiet Time*, p. 3. c) **Shoemaker**: *The Gospel According to You* (New York: Fleming H. Revell, 1934), pp. 81-91. d) **A.A.**: Big Book, pp. 84-88.

[18] a) **Bible**: Psalm 32:8. b) **Oxford Group**: Benson, *The Eight Points*, p. 80. c) **Shoemaker**: *With the Holy Spirit and with Fire*, pp. 30-31; *The Conversion of the Church*, p. 86; *Twice-Born Ministers*, pp. 184-85. d) **A.A.**: Big Book, Step Eleven.

[19] a) **Bible**: John 8:44; Matthew 5:5; Luke 14:33; John 13:34. b) **Oxford Group**: Robert E. Speer, *The Principles of Jesus* (New York: Fleming H. Revell, 1902), pp. 33-34; Garth Lean, *On the Tail of a Comet* (Colorado Springs: Helmers & Howard, 1988), p. 76. c) **Shoemaker**: *Twice-Born Ministers*, p. 150; *The Church Can Save the World*, p. 110; *How to Become a Christian*, p. 57. d) **A.A.**: *DR. BOB*, pp. 54, 163; *Pass It On*, pp. 114, 172; *Alcoholics Anonymous Comes of Age*, pp. 68, 161; *The Language of the Heart*, pp. 198-200; *The Co-Founders of Alcoholics Anonymous* (New York: Alcoholics Anonymous World Services, Inc., 1972), pp. 13-14; Mel B., *New Wine*, pp. 76, 138; Kurtz, *Not-God*, pp. 242-43.

[20] a) **Bible**: Psalm 46:10. b) **Oxford Group**: Benson, *The Eight Points*, pp. 58-73. c) **Shoemaker**: *Realizing Religion*, pp. 65-66. d) **A.A.**: Big Book, p. 86.

21. *Bible study*—Meditation which enables man daily to feed his soul on God's revelation of His Universal Will in the written Word.[21]

22. *Prayer*—Talking to God.[22]

23. *Listening to God for Leading Thoughts and Writing Down Guidance Received*—The means of receiving revelation of God's Particular or Private Will for a man.[23]

24. *Checking*—Testing thoughts to be sure they represent God's Guidance and not just self-deception.[24]

The Spiritual Experience or Awakening.

25. *Knowledge of God's will*—Attaining, with the Guidance of the Holy Spirit, a knowledge of God's Universal Will as revealed in the Bible, and receiving knowledge of His particular Will through obedience to His Universal Will.[25]

26. *God-consciousness*—The total change resulting from the experience of God when His will is known, lived, and witnessed.[26]

---

[21] a) **Bible**: 2 Timothy 2:15. b) **Oxford Group**: Streeter, *The God Who Speaks*; Russell, *For Sinners Only*, p. 94. c) **Shoemaker**: *Realizing Religion*, pp. 58-62; *The Conversion of the Church*, pp. 49, 60, 79; *Children of the Second Birth*, p. 97; *Twice-Born Ministers*, p. 184. d) **A.A.**: *DR. BOB*, pp. 71, 96-97, 102, 111, 116, 136, 139, 140, 144, 148, 151, 162, 183, 187, 198, 218, 224, 228, 252, 261, 276, 306, 308, 310, 311, 314.

[22] a) **Bible**: James 5:16. b) **Oxford Group**: *What Is The Oxford Group?*, p. 69. c) **Shoemaker**: *Realizing Religion*, pp. 63-65; *National Awakening*, p. 53; *Children of the Second Birth*, p. 149. d) **A.A.**: Big Book, p. 85.

[23] a) **Bible**: Jeremiah 30:1-2; 1 Samuel 3:9. b) **Oxford Group**: Buchman, *Remaking the World*, p. 36; H. Rose, *The Quiet Time*. c) **Shoemaker**: *The Conversion of the Church*, pp. 60-66; *Children of the Second Birth*, p. 47. d) **A.A.**: Big Book, pp. 86-87.

[24] a) **Bible**: John 16:13. b) **Oxford Group**: Russell, *For Sinners Only*, p. 94. c) **Shoemaker**: *The Conversion of the Church*, pp. 51-57; *Twice-Born Ministers*, p. 125. d) **A.A.**: *Alcoholics Anonymous Comes of Age*, p. 74; *Pass It On*, p. 172; *Co-Founders*, pp. 12-13.

[25] a) **Bible**: John 7:17; Acts 9:6. b) **Oxford Group**: Wright, *The Will of God*, p. 137. c) **Shoemaker**: *The Conversion of the Church*, pp. 49-50; *Twice-Born Ministers*, pp. 184-85; *A Young Man's View of the Ministry* (New York: Association Press, 1923), pp. 78, 80; *Religion That Works*, p. 36. d) **A.A.**: Big Book, Step Eleven.

[26] a) **Bible**: John 3:7; Matthew 10:39; Matthew 6:33; Acts 2:1,4. b) **Oxford Group**: Dick B., *The Oxford Group*, pp. 265-78. c) **Shoemaker**: Dick B., *The Oxford Group*, pp. 265-78. d) **A.A.**: Big Book, Step Twelve, pp. 569-70.

Fellowship with God and Believers and Witness by Life and Word.

27. *Fellowship*—The Fellowship of the Holy Spirit in which believers maintain fellowship with God and mutually sacrifice to win others to the fellowship of the love of God revealed by Jesus Christ.[27]

28. *Witness by Life and Word*—Sharing with others by personal evangelism the fruits of the life changed and the proof of God's forgiveness and power.[28]

---

[27] a) **Bible**: 1 John 1:3; Ephesians 2:1-22. b) **Oxford Group**: Benson, *The Eight Points*, pp. 102-13; c) **Shoemaker**: *Religion That Works*, pp. 66-76. d) **A.A.**: Big Book, p. 164.

[28] a) **Bible**: Acts 5:32; 26:22-23. b) **Oxford Group**: *What Is the Oxford Group?*, pp. 36, 26. c) **Shoemaker**: *One Boy's Influence* (New York: Association Press, 1925), p. 15; *They're on the Way*, p. 159; *How to Become a Christian*, p. 80. d) **A.A.**: Big Book Step Twelve.

Index

G

H

I

J

K

L

M

N

S

T

Y

Dick B.'s Historical Titles on Early A.A.'s Spiritual Roots and Successes

Dr. Bob and His Library: A Major A.A. Spiritual Source (Third Edition)

Foreword by Ernest Kurtz, Ph.D., Author, *Not-God: A History of Alcoholics Anonymous*.

A study of the immense spiritual reading of the Bible, Christian literature, and Oxford Group books done and recommended by A.A. co-founder, Dr. Robert H. Smith. Paradise Research Publications, Inc.; 156 pp.; 6 x 9; perfect bound; $15.95; 1998; ISBN 1-885803-25-7.

Anne Smith's Journal, 1933-1939: A.A.'s Principles of Success (Third Edition)

Foreword by Robert R. Smith, son of Dr. Bob & Anne Smith; co-author, *Children of the Healer*.

Dr. Bob's wife, Anne, kept a journal in the 1930's from which she shared with early AAs and their families ideas from the Bible and the Oxford Group. Her ideas substantially influenced A.A.'s program. Paradise Research Publications, Inc.; 180 pp.; 6 x 9; perfect bound; 1998; $16.95; ISBN 1-885803-24-9.

The Oxford Group & Alcoholics Anonymous (Second Edition)

Foreword by Rev. T. Willard Hunter; author, columnist, Oxford Group activist.

A comprehensive history of the origins, principles, practices, and contributions to A.A. of "A First Century Christian Fellowship" (also known as the Oxford Group) of which A.A. was an integral part in the developmental period between 1931 and 1939. Paradise Research Publications, Inc.; 432 pp.; 6 x 9; perfect bound; 1998; $17.95; ISBN 1-885803-19-2. (Previous title: *Design for Living*).

The Akron Genesis of Alcoholics Anonymous (Newton Edition)

Foreword by former U.S. Congressman John F. Seiberling of Akron, Ohio.

The story of A.A.'s birth at Dr. Bob's Home in Akron on June 10, 1935. Tells what early AAs did in their meetings, homes, and hospital visits; what they read; how their ideas developed from the Bible, Oxford Group, and Christian literature. Depicts roles of A.A. founders and their wives; Henrietta Seiberling; and T. Henry Williams. Paradise Research Pub.; 400 pp., 6 x 9; perfect bound; 1998; $17.95; ISBN 1-885803-17-6.

The Books Early AAs Read for Spiritual Growth (Fwd. by John Seiberling; 7th Ed.)

The most exhaustive bibliography (with brief summaries) of all the books known to have been read and recommended for spiritual growth by early AAs in Akron and on the East Coast. Paradise Research Publications, Inc.; 126 pp.; 6 x 9; perfect bound; 1998; $15.95; ISBN 1-885803-26-5.

New Light on Alcoholism: The A.A. Legacy from Sam Shoemaker

Forewords by Nickie Shoemaker Haggart, daughter of Rev. Sam Shoemaker; and Mrs. W. Irving Harris.

A comprehensive history and analysis of the all-but-forgotten specific contributions to A.A. spiritual principles and practices by New York's famous Episcopal preacher, the Rev. Dr. Samuel M. Shoemaker, Jr.—dubbed by Bill W. a "co-founder" of A.A. and credited by Bill as the well-spring of A.A.'s spiritual recovery ideas. Good Book Publishing Company; 416 pp.; 6 x 9; perfect bound; 1994; $19.95; ISBN 1-881212-06-8.

The Good Book and The Big Book: A.A.'s Roots in the Bible (Bridge Builders Ed.)

Foreword by Robert R. Smith, son of Dr. Bob & Anne Smith; co-author, *Children of the Healer*.

The author shows conclusively that A.A.'s program of recovery came primarily from the Bible. This is a history of A.A.'s biblical roots as they can be seen in A.A.'s Big Book, Twelve Steps, and Fellowship. Paradise Research Publications, Inc.; 264 pp.; 6 x 9; perfect bound; 1997; $17.95; ISBN 1-885803-16-8.

That Amazing Grace: The Role of Clarence and Grace S. in Alcoholics Anonymous

Foreword by Harold E. Hughes, former U.S. Senator from, and Governor of, Iowa.

Precise details of early A.A.'s spiritual practices—from the recollections of Grace S., widow of A.A. pioneer, Clarence S. Paradise Research Pub; 160 pp.; 6 x 9; perfect bound; 1996; $16.95; ISBN 1-885803-06-0.

Good Morning!: Quiet Time, Morning Watch, Meditation, and Early A.A.

A practical guide to Quiet Time—considered a "must" in early A.A. Discusses biblical roots, history, helpful books, and how to. Paradise Research Pub; 154 pp.; 6 x 9; perfect bound; 1998; $15.50; ISBN: 1-885803-09-5.

Turning Point: A History of Early A.A.'s Spiritual Roots and Successes

Foreword by Paul Wood, Ph.D., President, National Council on Alcoholism and Drug Dependence.

Turning Point is a comprehensive history of early A.A.'s spiritual roots and successes. It is the culmination of six years of research, traveling, and interviews. Dick B.'s latest title shows specifically what the Twelve Step pioneers borrowed from: (1) The Bible; (2) The Rev. Sam Shoemaker's teachings; (3) The Oxford Group; (4) Anne Smith's Journal; and (5) meditation periodicals and books, such as *The Upper Room*. Paradise Research Publications, Inc.; 776 pp.; 6 x 9; perfect bound; 1997; $29.95; ISBN: 1-885803-07-9.

How to Order Dick B.'s Historical Titles on Early A.A.

Order Form

Qty.	Title	Price	
Send: __	*Turning Point* (a comprehensivehistory)	@ $29.95 ea.	$______
__	*New Light on Alcoholism* (Sam Shoemaker)	@ $19.95 ea.	$______
__	*The Oxford Group & Alcoholics Anonymous*	@ $17.95 ea.	$______
__	*The Good Book and The Big Book* (Bible roots)	@ $17.95 ea.	$______
__	*The Akron Genesis of Alcoholics Anonymous*	@ $17.95 ea.	$______
__	*That Amazing Grace* (Clarence and Grace S.)	@ $16.95 ea.	$______
__	*Good Morning!* (Quiet Time, etc.)	@ $16.95 ea.	$______
__	*Anne Smith's Journal, 1933-1939*	@ $16.95 ea.	$______
__	*Books Early AAs Read for Spiritual Growth*	@ $15.95 ea.	$______
__	*Dr. Bob and His Library*	@ $15.95 ea.	$______

Shipping and Handling **(S & H) **** Subtotal $______

Add 10% of retail price (minimum US$3.75). ** U.S. only.
For "The Set," add US$18.67. ** U.S. only
Please call, fax, or email for shipments outside the U.S.

S & H $______

Total Enclosed $______

Name: ______________________________ (as it appears on your credit card)

Address: ______________________________

City: ______________________________ State: ____ Zip: __________

Credit Card #: ______________________________ (MC VISA AMEX) **Exp.** _____

Tel. #: ______________________________ Signature ______________________

Email address: ______________________________

Special Value for You!

If purchased separately, the author's ten titles sell for US$186.70, plus Shipping and Handling. Using this Order Form, you may purchase sets of all ten titles for **only $149.95 per set, plus US$18.67** Shipping and Handling. Please contact us for Shipping and Handling charges for orders being shipped outside of the United States.

Send Order Form (or copy), with check or money order, to: Dick B., P.O. Box 837, Kihei, HI 96753-0837. Please make check or money order payable to "**Dick B.**" in U.S. dollars drawn on a U.S. bank. For questions, please phone or fax: 1-808-874-4876. Our email: dickb@dickb.com. **Dick B.'s Web Site**: "http://www.dickb.com".